Nick Vandome

Windows 8.1

In easy steps is an imprint of In Easy Steps Limited
16 Hamilton Terrace · Holly Walk · Leamington Spa
Warwickshire · United Kingdom · CV32 4LY
www.ineasysteps.com

Notice of Liability
Every effort has been made to ensure that this book contains accurate
and current information. However, In Easy Steps Limited and the
author shall not be liable for any loss or damage suffered by readers
as a result of any information contained herein.

Trademarks
Microsoft® and Windows® are registered trademarks of Microsoft
Corporation. All other trademarks are acknowledged as belonging to
their respective companies.

In Easy Steps Limited supports The Forest Stewardship Council (FSC),
the leading international forest certification organisation. All our titles
that are printed on Greenpeace approved FSC certified paper carry the
FSC logo.

MIX
Paper from
responsible sources
FSC® C020837

Printed and bound in the United Kingdom

ISBN 978-1-84078-614-9

Contents

1 Introducing Windows 8.1

This chapter explains what Windows is and shows how to get started with it, including using the Windows 8.1 interface, Charms, creating a Microsoft Account and touchscreen capabilities.

What is Windows?

Windows is an operating system for PCs (personal computers). The operating system is the software that organizes and controls all of the components (hardware and software) in your computer so that they integrate and work efficiently together.

The first operating system from Microsoft was known as MS-DOS (Microsoft Disk Operating System). This was a non-graphical, line-oriented, command-driven operating system, able to run only one application at a time.

The original Windows system was an interface manager that ran on top of the MS-DOS system, providing a graphical user interface and using clever processor and memory management to allow it to run more than one application or function at a time.

The basic element of Windows was its 'windowing' capability. A window (with a lower-case w) is a rectangular area used to display information or to run a program. Several windows can be opened at the same time so that you can work with multiple applications. This provided a dramatic increase in productivity, in comparison with the original MS-DOS.

Microsoft released four versions of this interface management Windows, with numerous intermediate versions, including:

- 1985 – Windows 1.0

- 1987 – Windows 2.0, 2.1 and 2.11

- 1990 – Windows 3.0, 3.1, 3.11 (Windows for Workgroups)

- 1995 – Windows 95, 98, 98 SE and Me (Millennium Edition)

The next version, Windows XP, was a full operating system in its own right. This was eventually followed by Windows Vista:

- 2001 – Windows XP (eXPerience) Home and Professional

- 2007 – Windows Vista Home, Home Premium, Ultimate etc

- 2009 – Windows 7 Starter, Home Premium, Ultimate etc

- 2012 – Windows 8 Starter, Pro, Enterprise and RT

The New icon pictured above indicates a new or enhanced feature introduced with the latest version of Windows 8.1.

About Windows 8.1

The latest version of Windows was released in October 2013.

- 2013 – Windows 8.1, Windows 8.1 Pro, Windows Enterprise and Windows RT

Windows 8.1 continues the developments made with Windows 8 in that it is designed to work equally well on touchscreen devices and traditional computers. The number of versions of Windows 8.1 remain consolidated too, compared with previous versions and there are three main options on offer.

The Windows logo was redesigned for Windows 8, to make it look more like a window and less like a flag, as in earlier versions.

Windows 8.1

This is the main consumer version of the software. It includes the updated Windows 8.1 interface, Windows 8.1 apps and Internet Explorer 11. You can upgrade to Windows 8.1 from Windows 8 as a free download from the Windows Store or from a disc. There is also a 'full version', which has to be paid for, but can be installed on a computer that has not previously had a version of Windows installed. The full version of Windows 8.1 costs $119.99 (£75).

Windows 8.1 Pro

This is targeted more towards the business user. It contains all of the features in the standard Windows 8.1 version plus added features for security encryption and PC management. As with the standard version it can be upgraded to for free from a version of Windows 8 Pro. The full version costs $199.99 (£125).

All prices are correct at the time of writing this book in October 2013.

Windows 8.1 Enterprise

This a similar version to Windows 8.1 Pro, but with enhanced features for mobile business working. It also takes advantage of the development of new apps for mobile working.

Windows 8.1 RT

This version of Windows 8.1 is only available pre-installed on PCs and tablets with ARM processors, which help with a lightweight design and improved battery life for mobile devices. The RT version also comes with a pre-installed version of Microsoft Office (Word, Excel, Powerpoint and OneNote) that is optimized for use on touchscreen devices.

Windows 8.1 Interface

Windows 8 was one of the most significant changes to the Windows operating system since Windows 95 helped redefine the way that we look at personal computers. This evolution continues with Windows 8.1, with the most radical element being the user interface. This will be the first view of Windows 8.1 and all of the elements are accessed through the brightly colored Start screen.

The Windows 8.1 interface defines one of the main purposes of Windows 8.1: it is an operating system designed for the mobile generation so it will work in the same way on a desktop, laptop or tablet computer. It is the same operating system for all of these devices and it is also possible to synchronize Windows 8.1 so that all of your settings and apps will be available over multiple devices through an online Microsoft Account.

Another innovation that continues with Windows 8.1 is the greater use of custom apps (applications) that are accessed from the Start screen. This is done through the colored tiles: each tile gives access to the relevant app. For instance, if you click or tap on the Photos app you will be able to view, organize and edit your photo files and folders. A lot of the Windows 8.1 apps are linked together too, so it is easy to share content through your apps. There are also a number of Windows 8.1 Charms that can be accessed at any point within Windows 8.1 to give a range of functionality. These can be accessed from the right-hand side of the screen.

Hot tip

The Windows 8.1 interface is also known as the Metro interface and will be referred to in this way at certain points throughout the book.

10

Don't forget

Windows 8.1 apps are designed to be used in full-screen mode and cannot be minimized in the traditional way with Windows programs.

Don't forget

For a detailed look at working with the Windows 8.1 Charms see Chapter Two.

...cont'd

Windows 8.1 is also optimized for touchscreen use, so it is ideal for using with a tablet (such as the Microsoft Surface 2) where all of the screen navigation can be done by tapping, swiping and pinching on the screen. These features can also be used on desktops and laptops that have this functionality.

Even though Windows 8.1 has a very modern look with the Windows 8.1 interface, the old favorites such as the Desktop are not far away. The Desktop and all of its functionality that users have got used to with previous versions of Windows is available at the click or tap of a button and this takes you into an environment that, initially, may be more familiar.

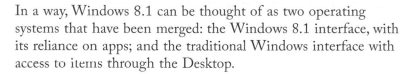

In a way, Windows 8.1 can be thought of as two operating systems that have been merged: the Windows 8.1 interface, with its reliance on apps; and the traditional Windows interface with access to items through the Desktop.

Most leading laptop manufacturers now have a range of touchscreen laptops, such as the Acer Aspire S7 and S5, HP's Envy TouchSmart and Spectre and Sony's VAIO T and VAIO E series. There are also various tablets and hybrids, which are tablets with docking and keyboard facilities.

11

It can take a little time getting used to working with the two interfaces.

Navigating Windows 8.1

Since Windows 8.1 is optimized for use with touchscreen devices this introduces a new factor when it comes to navigating around the system, particularly the new Windows 8.1 interface. The three ways of doing this are:

- Mouse

- Keyboard

- Touch

Some of these methods can be used in conjunction with each other (for instance mouse and keyboard, and touch and keyboard) but the main ways of getting around Windows 8.1 with each are:

Mouse

- Move the mouse to the bottom left-hand corner to access the Start button. Click or tap on it to go back to the Metro Start screen, or right-click on it to access a menu with more options, including those for shutting down

- Move the cursor over the top or bottom right-hand corners to access the Charms bar. Move down and click on one to access it

The Start button was not available in Windows 8, but it has been reinstated in Windows 8.1.

...cont'd

- Move the cursor over the top left-hand corner to view the most recently-used app. Click on it to access it

- Move the cursor over the top left-hand corner and drag down the left-hand side to view all of the currently-open apps (App Switcher). Click on one to access it

- In an open Windows 8.1 app, right-click to access the bottom toolbar. This will have options specific to the app in use

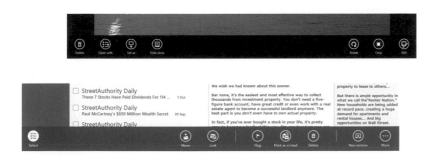

- In an open Windows 8.1 app, click and hold at the top of the window and drag down to the bottom of the screen to close the app

Hot tip

You can also close a Windows 8.1 app with the mouse by accessing the App Switcher and right-clicking on one of the apps and then clicking on the **Close** button.

13

...cont'd

Keyboard

The majority of the keyboard shortcuts for navigating around Windows 8.1 are accessed in conjunction with the WinKey. Press:

- **WinKey** to access the Start screen at any time

- **WinKey** + **L** to lock the computer and display the Lock screen

- **WinKey** + **C** to access the Charms bar

- **WinKey** + **I** to access the Settings Charm

- **WinKey** + **K** to access the Devices Charm

- **WinKey** + **H** to access the Sharing Charm

- **WinKey** + **Q** to access the Search Charm to search over apps

- **WinKey** + **F** to access the Search Charm to search over files

- **WinKey** + **D** to access the Desktop

- **WinKey** + **M** to access the Desktop with the active window minimized

- **WinKey** + **E** to access File Explorer, displaying the Computer folder

- **WinKey** + **T** to display the thumbnails on the Desktop Taskbar

- **WinKey** + **U** to access the Ease of Access Center

- **WinKey** + **X** to access administration tools and quick access to items including the Desktop and the Control Panel

- **WinKey** + **Z** in a Windows 8.1 app to display the app's toolbar at the bottom of the screen

- **Alt** + **F4** to close a Windows 8.1 app

- **Ctrl** + **Shift** + **Esc** to access the Task Manager

Touch

To navigate around Windows 8.1 with a touchscreen device:

- Tap on an item to access it

- Swipe inwards from the right-hand edge to access the Charms bar

- Swipe inwards from the left-hand edge to switch between currently-open apps

- Swipe inwards slowly from the left-hand edge and drag one of the apps away from the App Switcher to snap it to the left-hand side

- Swipe inwards from the left and then back again to show the currently-open apps (App Switcher)

- In an open Windows 8.1 app, swipe upwards from the bottom of the screen, or downwards from the top of the screen, to access the app's toolbar

- In an open Windows 8.1 app, swipe down from inside the app to view its settings

- In an open Windows 8.1 app, hold at the top of the screen and drag down to the bottom to close the app

- On the Start screen, swipe down on an app's tile to view additional options relating to the app

- Pinch outwards to minimize the Start screen. Pinch inwards to return to normal view

To perform a right-click operation on a Windows 8.1 touchscreen device, such as a tablet, tap and hold on an item on the screen until a contextual menu appears. This will contain the options that you can perform for the selected item.

15

Swipe left or right on the screen to move through the Start screen.

The Microsoft Account, and related services, replaces the Windows Live function. However, there will still be remnants of this online for some time and login details for this can be used for the Microsoft Account services.

Without a Windows Account you will not be able to access the apps listed here.

Microsoft Account details can also be used as your sign-in for Windows 8.1 (see pages 18-19).

Using a Microsoft Account

We live in a world of ever-increasing computer connectivity, where users expect to be able to access their content wherever they are and share it with their friends and family in a variety of ways, whether it is by email, messaging or photo sharing. This is known as cloud computing, with content being stored on online servers, from where it can be accessed by authorized users.

In Windows 8.1 this type of connectivity is achieved with a Microsoft Account. This is a registration system (which can be set up with most email addresses and a password) that provides access to a number of services via the Windows 8.1 apps. These include:

- **Mail.** This is the Windows 8.1 email app that can be used to access and manage your different email accounts

- **Skype.** This is the text messaging app

- **People.** This is the address book app

- **Calendar.** This is the calendar and organizer app

- **The Windows Store.** This is the online store for previewing and downloading additional apps

- **SkyDrive.** This is the online sharing service

Creating a Microsoft Account

It is free to create a Microsoft Account and can be done with an online email address and, together with a password, this provides a unique identifier for logging into your Microsoft Account and the related apps. There are several ways in which you can create and set up a Microsoft Account:

- During the initial setup process when you install Windows 8.1. You will be asked if you want to create a Microsoft Account at this point. If you do not, you can always do so at a later time

- When you first open an app that requires access to a Microsoft Account. When you do this you will be prompted to create a new account

- From the **Accounts** section of the **PC settings** that are accessed from the Settings Charm (for more information about the PC settings see Chapter Two, pages 50-53)

Whichever way you use to create a Microsoft Account the process
is similar:

1 When you are first prompted
to Sign in with a Microsoft
Account, click or tap on the
**Sign up for a Microsoft
account** link

2 Enter an email
address and a
password

3 Click or tap on the **Next** button to
move through the registration process

4 Enter additional
information including
your name, location and
zip/post code. On the
next screen you also
need to enter a phone
number, which is used
as a security measure by
Microsoft if you forget
your password

5 Click or tap on the
Finish button to
complete setting up your
Microsoft Account

If you create a Microsoft
Account when accessing
a related app, the sign-
up process will take you
to the online Account
Live web page, but the
process is similar. In both
cases you will be able
to log in to the Account
Live web page too, at
https://login.live.com
You can also access your
account details through
https://account.live.com

17

For details about personalizing the Lock screen see Chapter Two.

Hot tip

You can lock your PC at any point by pressing the **WinKey + L**.

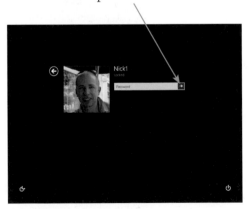

Don't forget

You will get an error message if you enter the wrong password or if you simply mis-key and cause an incorrect character to be added.

Sign-in Options

Each time you start up your computer you will need to sign in. This is a security feature so that no-one else can gain unauthorized access to your account on your PC. This sign-in process starts with the Lock screen and then you have to enter your login password.

1 When you start your PC the Lock screen will be showing. This can only be opened by your password

2 Click or tap on the **Lock screen**, or press any key, to move to the login screen. Enter your password and press **Enter** or click or tap on this arrow

3 On the login screen, click or tap on this button to select Ease of Access options

4 Click or tap on this button to select Power off options including Shut Down and Restart

5 On the login screen, click or tap on this button to view the login screen for all users on the PC

6 Click or tap on another user to access their own login screen

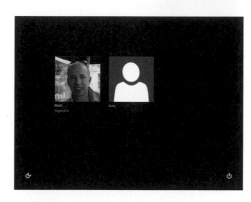

You can sign in with a local account or a Microsoft Account. If you sign in with the latter you will have access to the related services, such as Mail, Messaging and People. Also, you will be able to sync your settings and use them from another computer if you log in there with your Microsoft Account.

Login settings

Settings for how you log in can be accessed from the Users section in the PC settings:

1 Access the PC settings and click or tap on the **Accounts** button

2 Under **Sign-in options**, select options to change your password, create a picture password or create a PIN instead of a password

For details about accessing and using PC settings see Chapter Two.

3 If you want to create a picture password you must have a touchscreen device. Select a picture and draw a pattern to use as your login

PC Requirements

The recommended specifications for PCs running Windows 8.1 are based on the processor mode used. On most current processors, you have the choice of 32-bit or 64-bit mode.

Windows 8.1 for 32-bit Processor Mode
The PC should have these minimum hardware requirements:

- Processor   1GHz
- System Memory   1GB
- Graphics   SVGA (800 x 600)
- Graphics adapter   DirectX9 class with WDDM 1.0 driver
- Graphics memory   128MB (for Aero support)
- Hard Disk   16GB available space
- Other   DVD-RW optical drive

Windows 8.1 for 64-bit Processor Mode
The PC should have these minimum hardware requirements:

- Processor   1GHz
- System Memory   2GB
- Graphics   SVGA (800 x 600)
- Graphics adapter   DirectX9 class with WDDM 1.0 driver
- Graphics memory   128MB (for Aero support)
- Hard Disk   20GB
- Other   DVD-RW optical drive

Windows Virtual PC requires a PC with Intel-VT or AMD-V enabled in the CPU, since the software relies on hardware virtualization features.

If you want to upgrade your existing PC to run Windows 8.1, you can run the Windows 8.1 Upgrade Assistant to identify any potential problems or short-comings.

Don't forget

These are the supported specifications. However, Windows 8.1 will work with virtually any graphics hardware that supports Windows XP or later.

Hot tip

Additional hardware includes a pointing device such as a mouse, a sound card and speakers. Note that BitLocker Drive Encryption requires a TPM 1.2 chip or a USB 2.0 flash drive.

32-Bit versus 64-Bit

As well as choosing your Windows 8.1 edition, you also need to decide between the 32-bit and the 64-bit versions of the operating system. This choice is available for all editions of Windows 8.1 with the retail packs including installation DVDs for each mode.

The 32-bit or 64-bit nomenclature refers to the memory address length which the processor can reference. This dictates the maximum amount of memory, which is 4GB for 32-bit mode (or more exactly 3.4GB, since some memory needs to be allocated to other purposes). For 64-bit mode, the maximum may be much higher, though the Windows 8.1 editions do not make full use of the potential. As well as more memory, 64-bit mode will also be faster, typically about 10%.

However, you need applications that are specifically optimized for 64-bit processing to take advantage of the speed improvements and memory increase. Many games, for example, include the necessary enhancements.

Remember that choosing a 64-bit system means that you can no longer run 16-bit applications. This is only a problem if you use very old software (from the Windows 3.1 days).

More seriously, existing 32-bit drivers for your devices will not operate in 64-bit mode, so you will have to locate 64-bit versions of the drivers. You may have problems with some devices, particularly the older ones.

You may also find that running 32-bit applications in a 64-bit operating system might actually be slower, due to the additional overheads imposed by conversion between the address systems.

In summary, if you have a 64-bit capable computer but use older hardware or 32-bit applications, you might do better to stay with the 32-bit version of Windows 8.1. With the latest hardware and drivers, and applications that are 64-bit optimized, for especially demanding applications such as video editing or image packages, the switch to 64-bit and higher memory would offer significant improvements.

It will not be long before 64-bit computing becomes the standard, and 32-bit operation becomes an optional extra, but for the present there are still large numbers of 32-bit applications.

Beware

If your computer is more than a few years old, it is quite possible that you can only run the 32-bit version of Windows 8.1.

It is free to upgrade from Windows 8 to 8.1. You can also buy the full version: this can be downloaded from www. windows.com

There is also a packaged DVD version available. This is the full version of Windows 8.1 and does not require a previous copy of Windows for installation. As already mentioned from October 2013 the price for the download and packaged version of Windows 8.1 is $119.99 (approx. £75).The Pro version is $199.99 (approx. £125). *(Prices correct at the time of printing.)*

If you are upgrading from Windows 7 you will be able to keep all of your settings, files and apps.

Installing Windows 8.1

As with many things to do with Windows 8.1, the installation process has been simplified as much as possible. Depending on how you have obtained Windows 8.1 the options are:

- **Upgrade** – Replace an older version of Windows, retaining the installed applications and settings. This can only be done with Windows 7 and later: for earlier version you will need to install a new, full, copy of Windows 8.1. **If you already have Windows 8 it is free to upgrade to Windows 8.1**

- **Dual Boot** – Install Windows 8.1 while retaining the existing version of Windows, using a second disk partition. You'll need to install required applications to the new system

- **Clean Install** – This has to be done if you have Windows XP or Windows Vista and you want to upgrade to Windows 8.1 This has to be done with the full version of Windows 8.1

- **Pre-install** – Buy a new PC with Windows 8.1 already installed, then install the required apps

In previous versions of Windows there was an Upgrade Advisor that checked your PC to see if there were any issues with regard to updating to the next version of Windows. However, with Windows 8.1 this is all incorporated into the Windows 8.1 Setup process itself. If you are upgrading from a previous version of Windows there is a Windows 8.1 Upgrade Assistant that will help with the installation process. Initially it will check the compatibility of your current setup and apps and flag up any issues. Then the installation will go through the following steps:

- **Product key.** This will be needed if you install your copy of Windows 8.1 from a DVD

- **Personalize.** These are settings that will be applied to your version of Windows 8.1. They include the color for the Start screen, a name for your computer and a connection to a wireless network. These settings can be selected within PC Settings once Windows 8.1 has been installed too

- **Settings.** You can choose to have express settings applied, or customize them

- **Microsoft Account.** You can set up a Microsoft Account during installation, or once you have started Windows 8.1

2 Getting Started

Windows 8.1 improves upon the radical design of Windows 8 and places Windows very firmly in the mobile computing environment. Many of its features are inspired by the Windows Phone interface. This chapter looks at some of the main features of Windows 8.1, focusing on the Start screen and the Metro interface. It shows how to navigate around these and organize them so that you can quickly feel comfortable using Windows 8.1.

The Start Screen

One of the most radical changes in Windows 8 was the Start screen and this has been continued with Windows 8.1, albeit with some enhancements. There are greater personalization options for the Start screen, and the Start button, which was removed in Windows 8, has been reinstated (see page 26). Even so, the Start screen remains a considerable departure from earlier versions of Windows and is a significant learning curve for new users.

The Start screen is a collection of large, brightly colored tiles. By default these are the apps (programs) which are provided with Windows 8.1. Although the Start screen is a big change from previous Windows' interfaces there is considerable functionality for finding items, getting around and customizing your Windows 8.1 experience. Also, it is still possible to access your old Windows favorites such as the Desktop and the Control Panel.

First view

Once you sign in from the Lock screen the Start screen is the first thing you will see:

The Windows 8.1 apps are shown as colored tiles. These are the built-in apps that have been designed specifically for use with Windows 8.1. Much of the functionality of the Start screen works best with these apps.

Don't forget

It may take a little time to get used to the new Start screen compared to previous versions of Windows. However, the more you use it the more you will begin to exploit the potential of this ground-breaking version of Windows.

...cont'd

Another change in Windows 8 was that the scroll bars were not visible by default and this has continued with Windows 8.1. However, they are still there and can be used to view the rest of the apps on the Start screen: The scroll bars appear when you move the cursor on the Start screen.

1 Click on the scroll bar at the bottom of the screen and scroll to the right to view all of the apps on the Start screen. Scroll back to the left as required

When you are working in any app, the Start screen can be accessed at any time by moving the cursor over the bottom left-hand corner of the screen. When the Start button icon appears, click or tap on it to move to the Start screen. On the Desktop, the Start button is always visible on the Taskbar.

Beware

Move the cursor fully into the bottom left-hand corner to access the Start button icon. Click or tap on the icon while the cursor still feels as if it has gone off the edge of the screen. If you move the cursor first then the Start button icon may disappear.

The Start Button is Back

One of the biggest criticisms of Windows 8 was that the old favorite of the Windows operating system, the Start button, had been removed. Although this was replaced by a button to return to the Start screen, it did not meet with approval from a lot of users. In Windows 8.1 this has been rectified with the return of the Start button, although it still does not have the old Start Menu that was previously accessed from the Start button.

Accessing the Start button

The Start button is not always visible from the Start screen or the new Windows app, but can be accessed by moving the cursor over the bottom left-hand corner.

On the Desktop the Start button is pinned to the Taskbar in the left-hand corner.

Using the Start button

The Start button functions slightly differently, depending on whether you are in Metro or Desktop mode:

1 From the Start screen, click or tap on the **Start** button to go to the most recently used app (this will also be the Desktop if this was the most recently used item)

2 From a Metro app, click or tap on the **Start** button to go back to the Start screen

3 From the Desktop, click or tap on the **Start** button to go back to the Start screen

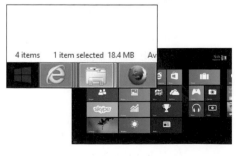

Start button functionality

Although the Start button is different to earlier versions of Windows, it still has a range of functionality:

1 Right-click, or press and hold, on the **Start** button to view its menu

Programs and Features
Mobility Centre
Power Options
Event Viewer
System
Device Manager
Network Connections
Disk Management
Computer Management
Command Prompt
Command Prompt (Admin)

Task Manager
Control Panel
File Explorer
Search
Run

Shut down or sign out   ▶
Desktop

Hot tip

Click or tap on the **Power Options** button in Step 1 to specify actions to be taken when you press your computer's power button.

2 Click or tap on the relevant buttons to view items including the **Desktop** and **Control Panel**

Control Panel
File Explorer
Search
Run

Shut down or sign out   ▶
Desktop

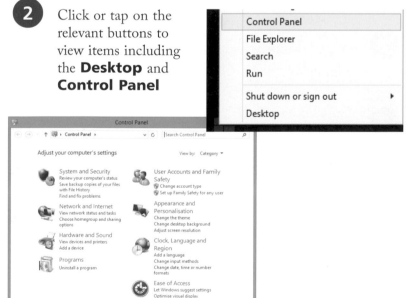

Don't forget

The Control Panel can also be accessed by clicking or tapping on the All Apps button on the Start screen and selecting it from the list that is available.

3 Shut down options have also been added to the **Start** button (see page 29)

The Desktop

The Desktop is still an integral part of Windows 8.1 and it can be accessed as shown on the previous page from the Start button, or from the Desktop tile on the Start screen:

1 On the Start screen, click or tap on the **Desktop** tile

2 Move the cursor over items on the Taskbar to see tooltips about the item. When apps are opened their icons appear on the Taskbar

3 The notifications area at the right-hand side of the Taskbar has speaker, network and other system tools. Click or tap on one to see more information about each item

Opening at the Desktop

If you do not like the Start screen interface, you can now specify that the Desktop appears when you start your computer:

1 In Desktop mode, right-click on the Taskbar at the bottom of the window. Click or tap on the **Properties** button

Properties

2 In the **Taskbar and Navigation properties** window, click or tap on the **Navigation** tab

3 Check on the **Go to the desktop instead of Start when I sign in** checkbox

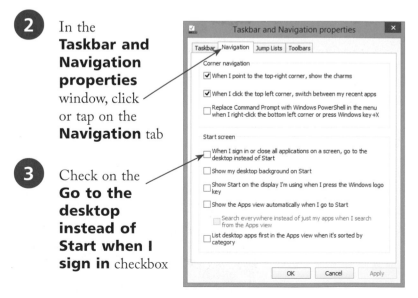

Shutting Down

The method of shutting down in Windows 8 was another contentious issue and one which has been addressed in Windows 8.1 by adding this functionality to the Start button as well as the previous method through the Settings Charm.

Shutting down from the Start button

1 Right-click, or press and hold, on the **Start** button and click or tap on the **Shut down** button

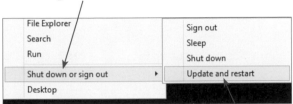

2 Click or tap on the **Sign out**, **Sleep**, **Shut down** or **Restart** options

Shutting down from the Settings Charm

1 Move the cursor over the bottom right-hand corner of the screen and click or tap on the **Settings Charm**

2 Click or tap on the **Power** button

3 Click or tap on the **Sleep**, **Shut down** or **Restart** options

For some updates to Windows you will need to restart your computer for them to take effect.

29

Around the Start Screen

In addition to accessing the default apps on the Start screen, there is also a range of functionality that can be accessed by moving the cursor over the edges and corners of the screen:

1 Move the cursor over the bottom or top right-hand corners to access the Charms bar. These are five icons that can be used for a variety of functions (see pages 42-45 to see details about the Charms)

The Charms bar can also be accessed by swiping in from the right-hand side of the screen on a touchscreen device, or using **WinKey** + **C** on a keyboard.

30

2 Click or tap on the bottom **Charm** (Settings) to access the relevant settings for the Start screen

For more information about the default Start screen settings see pages 46-47.

...cont'd

3 Move the cursor over the top left-hand corner to view the most recently-accessed app. Click or tap on it to access it

4 Drag down from the top left-hand corner to view all of the currently-open apps. Click or tap on one to access it

One option in Step 4 is the Desktop which displays the most recently-used item on the Desktop, regardless of how many apps are open there.

Organizing the Start Screen

By default, the Windows 8.1 apps are organized into different groups on the Start screen. These are mainly according to content type, e.g. communications or entertainment apps in different grouped columns for ease of access. However, it is possible to fully-customize the way that the apps are organized on the Start screen. To do this:

1 Move the cursor over the bottom right-hand corner and click or tap on this button to minimize the groups on the Start screen

Hot tip

Left-click anywhere on the Start screen to return it to full size from its minimized state (or pinch outwards on a touchscreen device).

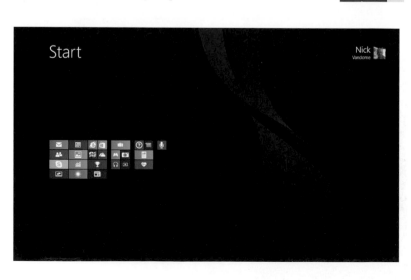

2 Click or tap and hold on a group to select it

3 Drag the group to move its position on the Start screen

Moving tiles

Tiles can be rearranged within their respective groups. To do this:

1 Click, or press, and hold on a tile and drag it into a new position in the group

2 The other tiles move to accommodate the tile in its new position

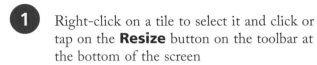

Resizing Tiles

As well as rearranging tiles, their sizes can also be edited on the Start screen. Depending on their original size, there are three options for resizing tiles in Windows 8.1: wide, large, medium and small. Initially, the tiles are a mixture of medium and wide:

1 Right-click on a tile to select it and click or tap on the **Resize** button on the toolbar at the bottom of the screen

2 For a medium size tile, tap on the **Small** option to reduce it in size

3 The tile is reduced in size and a gap appears next to it (unless there is another tile small enough to fill the space next to it)

...cont'd

4 For a wide tile, the options are for making it **Large**, **Medium** or **Small**

5 The **Large** size is the biggest available option for resizing tiles. Tiles that have been resized can be moved around the Start screen, but only to areas where there is enough space for them

The **Large** size is a good option for a tile that can then be used as a live tile to display its contents or real-time information.

6 Creating a range of different tile sizes is a good way to organize the Start screen and create a good mixture from a design point of view

Working with Groups

The default groups of apps can be expanded by creating new groups from the existing ones. This is done by dragging the app tiles out of their current groups to create new ones. To do this:

 Click, or tap, and hold on a tile and drag it away from its current group until a thick vertical line appears behind the tile

 Drag the tile into its new position to create a new group

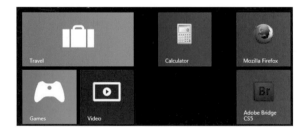

Naming Groups

In their initial state, groups on the Start screen are not named, but it is possible to give them all their own individual names or titles. To do this:

 Right-click on the Start screen and click or tap on the **Customize** button

2 Click or tap on the **Name group** button

3 Enter a name for the group and click on the Start screen

Don't forget

Group names can be edited with the same process as when creating them in the first place.

4 The name is applied at the top of the group

Side-by-Side Apps

In Windows 8 the Start screen apps could only be viewed
full screen, one at a time, or snapped to the side of the screen.
However, in Windows 8.1 you can have up to four apps visible on
the screen at the same time (depending on your screen resolution).
Once this has been done, the side-by-side apps create their own
window that can be accessed from the App Switcher. To create
and view side-by-side apps:

1 By default,
an app takes
up the full
screen

2 Swipe down from
the top left-hand
corner to view the
open apps in the
App Switcher

Hot tip

Right-click on an app on
the App Switcher and
select to insert it to the
left or the right of the
currently displayed app.

3 Drag the
required
app onto
the screen.
It can be
positioned
either side
of the
current app

...cont'd

4 Drag the middle dividing bar to determine how much of the screen each app uses

5 Drag more apps onto the screen (up to a maximum of four, depending on your screen resolution). The Desktop can also be included in this way. Click or tap on an app to make it the active one and use it in the usual way

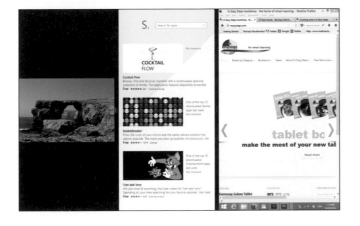

6 The side-by-side apps are grouped together and can be accessed as a group from the App Switcher in the same way as other apps

Beware

The side-by-side functionality does not work if only the Start screen is displayed in Windows 8.1, i.e. if you drag an app onto the Start screen the app will appear at full size.

Hot tip

To exit the side-by-side mode, drag the dividing bar to the side of the screen for one of the apps. This will make it full screen size.

39

Personalization

There are an increased number of options for personalizing the Start screen in Windows 8.1:

1 Access the Settings Charm and click on the **Personalize** button at the top of the panel

2 Click or tap on one of these thumbnails to select a background pattern

Don't forget

Each background has a default color scheme, but this can be changed by dragging the sliders in Steps 3 and 4.

3 Drag this slider to select a background color

4 Drag this slider to select an accent color that is applied to elements on the background

5 The selections in Steps 2, 3 and 4 are applied to the Start screen

Don't forget

Your geographic location will determine the spellings of certain terms (see tip on page 36).

Personalizing the Account Photo

To set your own photo for your personal account:

1 Click or tap on the **Accounts** link at the top of the **PC settings** page

2 Click or tap on the **Browse** button to select a picture for your account

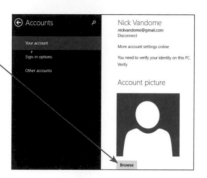

3 Select a photo or picture and click or tap on the **Choose image** button to add it as your account picture

The Account picture can also be changed by selecting your account name at the top right-hand corner of the screen and selecting the **Change account picture** link.

4 The photo is displayed on the Accounts screen

5 The photo is also displayed at the top right-hand corner of the Start screen where you can lock the screen or change users

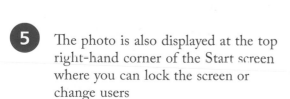

Working with Charms

As shown on the page 30, the Charms can be accessed by moving the cursor over the bottom or top right-hand corners of the screen. The Charms are, from top to bottom:

- Search
- Sharing
- Start screen
- Devices
- Settings

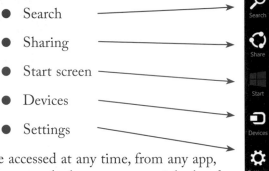

The Charms can be accessed at any time, from any app, by moving the cursor over the bottom or top right-hand corners of the screen. Therefore if you want to access, for instance, the Start screen while you are working in the Photos app this can be done with the Start screen Charm.

Settings

The Settings Charm can be used to access the Start screen settings and also PC settings for personalizing the Start screen (see page 40 for more details). It can also be accessed from any app and used for settings for that specific app. So, if you are working in the Mail app and select the Settings Charm, you will be provided with the Mail Settings. Or, if you are in Internet Explorer you will be provided with settings for this and so on. To use the Settings Charm:

1 Access the Charms and click or tap on the **Settings Charm**

2 At the bottom of the panel are the default settings that are always available from the Settings Charm

Don't forget

When you access the Charms bar, a separate panel displays the date, time, Wi-Fi connection and battery charge level (if using a laptop).

...cont'd

3 At the top of the panel are settings specific to the Start screen

4 Open an app and select the **Settings Charm**. The default settings are still available at the bottom of the panel, but the top now has settings options for the active app, i.e. the one currently being used. For example, these are the settings for Internet Explorer

Beware

The Devices Charm only works from compatible devices on the Start screen, but not the Desktop. For instance, the Photos app will usually have printer devices available, but if you open a word processing app, such as Word, on the Desktop then there will be no devices available from the Devices Charm. However, items such as printers can still be accessed from the app's Menu bar on the Desktop as in previous versions of Windows.

Devices

The Devices Charm can be used to send items in an app to any available device. For instance, if you are viewing a photo in the Photos app, you can use the Devices Charm to send it to any available printers. To use the Devices Charm:

1 Access the Charms and click or tap on the **Devices Charm**

2 Select a device. The related task will then be undertaken, i.e. an item will be sent to a printer

43

...cont'd

Start screen Charm

Click or tap on this Charm to return to the Start screen at any point from within Windows 8.1.

To use the Share Charm you have to first select an item in an appropriate app, i.e. select a photo in the Photos app, rather than just open the app.

Sharing Charm

The Sharing Charm can be used to share items within an app with the suite of apps, including Mail and People (the address book app). To use the Sharing Charm:

1 Access the Charms and click or tap on the **Sharing Charm**

2 Select the app with which you want to share the current content. This could involve emailing a photo to someone or sending a web page directly to a contact in the People app

44

...cont'd

Search Charm

The Search Charm can be used to search for items within the app in which you are working. For instance, if the Video app is open then the search will be conducted over this by default.

The Search Charm can also be used to search over your computer and your apps. To use the Search Charm:

1 Access the Charms and click on the **Search Charm**

2 Select an area over which you want to perform the search, e.g. Settings in this case

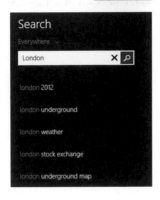

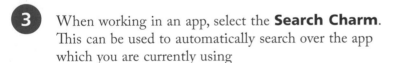

When you enter search words into the Search box, suggestions appear below, relating to the app over which you are performing the search.

45

3 When working in an app, select the **Search Charm**. This can be used to automatically search over the app which you are currently using

Charm Shortcuts

The individual Charms can also be accessed with keyboard shortcuts. These are:

- All Charms: **WinKey + C**
- Settings Charm: **WinKey + I**
- Devices Charm: **WinKey + K**
- Start screen: **WinKey**
- Sharing Charm: **WinKey + H**
- Search Charm: **WinKey + Q**

The WinKey is the one with the Windows icon on the keyboard.

Default Settings

As shown on page 42 some of the settings on the Settings Charm are available whenever this is accessed, regardless of which app you are in. To use these:

1 Access the Settings Charm by moving the cursor over the bottom or top right-hand corners and click or tap on this icon

2 The default settings appear at the bottom of the panel, above the Change PC settings link

3 Click or tap on this button to access Network and Wi-Fi settings

Hot tip

You can connect to, and disconnect from, network connections in the Networks Setting, by selecting the name of a network and selecting either the Connect or Disconnect button.

4 If you have moved to a level down in the Settings structure, click or tap on this button at the top of the panel to move back to the previous level

5 Click or tap on this button to adjust the volume. Drag this slider to make the adjustment

6 Click or tap on this button to adjust the screen brightness. Drag this slider to make the adjustment

Notifications can be set for a variety of apps so that you are alerted when there is new information. Settings for notifications can be selected within the **Search & apps > Notifications** section of the **PC settings**.

7 Click or tap on this button to specify timescales for when notifications appear

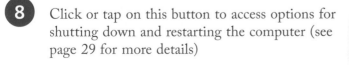

Hide for 8 hours

Hide for 3 hours

Hide for 1 hour

8 Click or tap on this button to access options for shutting down and restarting the computer (see page 29 for more details)

9 Click or tap on the keyboard button to view the current language

ENG
Keyboard

A virtual keyboard can be displayed by selecting **Change PC settings > Ease of Access > Keyboard** and dragging the **On-Screen Keyboard** button to On.

Lock Screen Settings

The Settings Charm enables you to set the appearance of the Lock screen, the Start screen and select an account photo. To do this, first access the PC settings:

1 Access the Charms and click or tap on the **Settings Charm**

2 Click or tap on the **Change PC settings** link

3 Click or tap on the **PC & devices** button underneath the PC settings heading

Personalizing the Lock screen

To personalize the Lock screen:

1 Click or tap on the **Lock screen** link at the top of the Personalize page

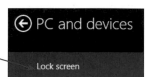

2 Click or tap on one of the thumbnail images to select a new image for the Lock screen

The Personalize PC settings only apply to the new interface elements of Windows 8.1, i.e. the Start screen, Lock screen and account photo. The Desktop can be personalized using the Control Panel as in previous versions of Windows. For more information about this see Chapter Five.

Drag the button to On underneath the Slide show heading to enable a slide show of your photos to be included on the Lock screen. Once this has been enabled you can choose a location from where you want to include photos.

48

...cont'd

3 The selected image becomes the Lock screen background

4 Click or tap on the **Browse** button to select an image from your hard drive for the Lock screen background

5 Select an image and click or tap on **Choose Image** to set the image as the Lock screen background

6 The image is added as the background for the Lock screen

PC Settings

Accessing settings

The PC Settings have been enhanced and expanded in Windows 8.1 so that all of the items that you might use in the Control Panel can be used here too. To access the PC Settings:

1 Access the Charms and click or tap on the **Settings Charm**

2 Click or tap on the **Change PC settings** link

3 Click or tap on one of the PC settings to view the options for that item

Don't forget

The main PC settings page displays the **Top Settings** if nothing is selected in Step 3. This lists the items that you have most recently viewed or edited within the PC settings section.

50

PC and devices

Select the **PC and devices** option to access settings for functionality of your Windows 8.1 device. This includes

Hot tip

In the **PC & devices** section, select the **Corners & edges** option to specify what happen when you move the cursor over the side of the screen or a corner.

settings for the Lock screen, the display, Bluetooth settings, adding devices, settings for the mouse and keyboard/touchpad, power and sleep options, AutoPlay options for when you add external devices and PC info which gives details about your computer and your version of Windows.

Accounts

Select the **Accounts**
option to access settings
for viewing your
own account details,
switching between a
Microsoft and a local
account, options for
how you sign in to your
account from the Lock
screen and a link for
adding other users to
your computer.

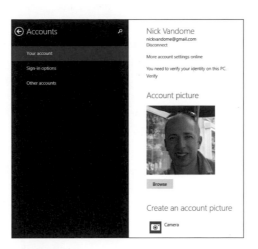

The Accounts settings
can be used to switch
between a Microsoft
Account and a local
account for signing in to
your PC.

SkyDrive

SkyDrive
is the online
storage and
sharing service
for Windows
users and these
settings show

your amount of storage space, options for the types of files stored
by SkyDrive and settings for syncing your computer settings with
SkyDrive so that they will be available on all of your compatible
devices and online.

Search and apps

Select the **Search
and apps** option
to access settings to
set search options,
such as a default
search engine on
your computer,
options for sharing
content from your
apps, notification
settings for specific
apps, the amount of
space being taken up

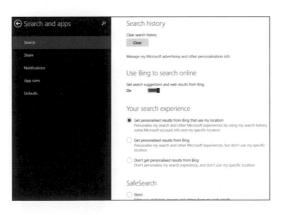

by your apps, and default apps for certain types of content.

...cont'd

Privacy

Select the **Privacy** button to access settings for letting selected apps use your geographical location over the Internet and also let them access

your account username and picture, if required. There are also options for allowing apps to use your webcam and microphone, if you have them installed.

Network

Select the **Network** button to access settings for connecting to Wi-Fi or Ethernet networks for access to the Internet, connecting to Bluetooth devices, Internet connection settings, options

for what you want to share over the HomeGroup network, and options for connecting to a workplace network.

Time and language

Select the **Time and language** button to access settings for specifying how the date and time is selected and displayed on your Windows 8.1 device. This can be done automatically or you can select to set it manually.

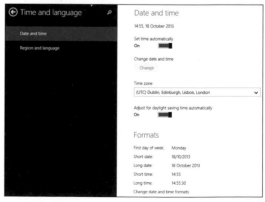

Don't forget

The date and time can be set within the Clock, Language, and Region section of the Control Panel, under the Date and Time heading.

Ease of Access

Select the **Ease of Access** button to select options for making the PC easier to use for people with visual or mobility issues. These include using the Narrator, for speaking what is on the screen, using the Magnifier to magnify what is on screen, the contrast of the screen, options for using the On-Screen Keyboard, and the size of the mouse pointer.

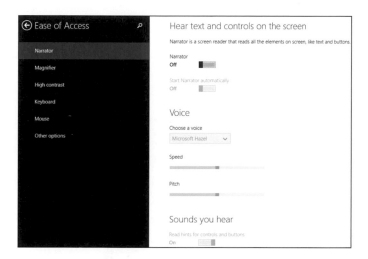

Update and recovery

Select the **Update and recovery** button to select options for how updates to Windows 8.1 are handled by your device. By default, they are set to be installed automatically, although this can be changed under **Windows Update > Choose how updates get installed**. There are also options for backing up certain file types and refreshing your PC or reinstalling Windows.

Security Options

There are a number of security options that can be set within Windows 8.1 to help protect your computer from viruses or malicious software. These are accessed through the Action Center.

When there are important alerts, an alert icon appears on the white flag in the notifications area on the Taskbar.

 Click or tap the **flag** for brief details of the message(s), click or tap on a specific message or click or tap on the **Open Action Center** link

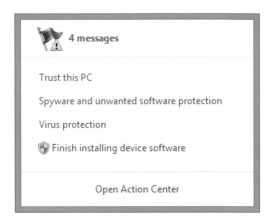

54

2 Security messages are color coded, with red being the most serious. Click on each item to undertake the required action to solve the problem

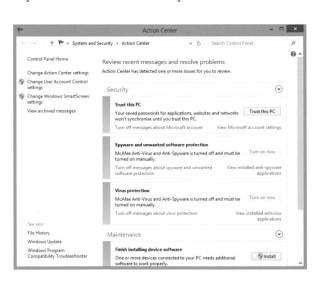

Help and Support Center

Help is at hand for Windows 8.1 through the Help and Support Center and also online resources:

1 Move the cursor over the bottom right-hand corner of the screen and click or tap on the **Settings Charm**

2 Click or tap on the **Help** link under the Settings heading

3 If the Help link is accessed in this way from the Start screen, this Help window is available. This takes you to online Help pages

4 If the Help link is accessed in this way from the Desktop, this Help window is available

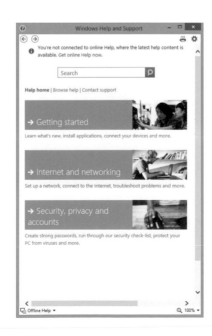

5 Click or tap on a link to view additional information about specific topics

Enter keywords into the Search box in Step 4 to look for specific items.

Adding Users

If more than one person uses the computer, each person can have a user account defined with a user name and a password. To create a new user account, as either a Microsoft Account, or as a local account.

1 Access the PC settings and select **Accounts**

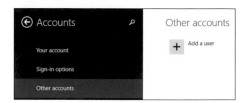

2 Under **Other accounts**, click or tap on the **Add a user** button

3 To add a user with a Microsoft Account, enter an email address

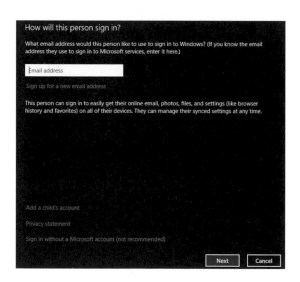

4 Click or tap on the **Next** button (see Step 10)

5 To create a local account, click or tap on the **Sign in without a Microsoft account** link

Sign in without a Microsoft account

6 At this stage you will still be encouraged to log in with a Microsoft Account and information about both types is displayed

7 Click or tap on the **Local account** button

8 Enter a user name, a password and a password hint in case the password is forgotten

Hot tip

Family Safety settings can be applied in the Family Safety section in the Control Panel. It is accessed under the User Accounts and Family Safety section. Click or tap on a user and then settings can be applied for items such as web filtering, time controls and app restrictions.

9 Select this box if it is a child's account and you want it to be monitored by the Family Safety feature

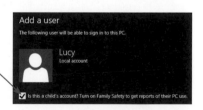

10 For a Microsoft Account, more information is required. Enter the relevant details in the fields and select the **Next** button to complete the additional windows in the registration process

57

Switching Users

If you have a number of user accounts defined on the computer (several accounts can be active at the same time) you do not need to close your apps and log off to be able to switch to another user and it is easy to switch back and forth.

Don't forget

All of your settings and files are maintained but the new user will not be able to see them; and you will not be able to see theirs when you switch back. Your screen will look exactly the same as you left it.

1 Click or tap on the name of the current active user in the top right-hand corner of the Start screen

2 Click on another user's name. They will have to enter their own password in order to access their account, at which point they will be signed in. You can then switch between users without each having to log out each time

As an alternative way to switch users:

1 Press **WinKey** + **L** to lock the current user

2 Access the login screen for all of the current users and select one as required

Beware

If the other accounts have data files open, shutting down without logging them off could cause them to lose information.

Shut Down
When you turn off your computer (see page 29), you will be warned if there are other user accounts still logged on to the computer.

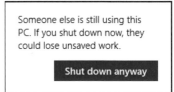

Someone else is still using this PC. If you shut down now, they could lose unsaved work.

Shut down anyway

1 Click or tap on the **Shut down anyway** button to shut down without other users logging off

3 Working with Apps

"Apps" is one of the new buzzwords in computing. Put simply it is just another name for computer programs. In Windows 8.1, some apps are pre-installed, as with previous versions of Windows, while hundreds more can be downloaded from the Windows Store. This chapter shows how to work with and organize apps in Windows 8.1 and how to find your way around the Windows Store.

Starting with Apps

The word "app" may be seen by some as a new-fangled piece of techno-speak. But, simply, it means a computer program. Originally, apps were items that were downloaded to smartphones and tablet computers. However, the terminology has now been expanded to cover any computer program. So, in Windows 8.1 most programs are referred to as "apps", although some legacy ones may still be referred to as "programs".

There are three clear types of apps within Windows 8.1:

- **Windows 8.1 apps.** These are the built-in apps that appear on the Start screen. They cover the areas of communication, entertainment and information and several of them are linked together through the online sharing service, SkyDrive.

- **Windows apps.** These are the old-style Windows apps that people may be familiar with from previous versions of Windows. These open in the Desktop environment.

- **Windows Store apps.** These are apps that can be downloaded from the online Windows Store, and cover a wide range of subjects and functionality. Some Windows Store apps are free while others have to be paid for.

Windows 8.1 apps

Windows 8.1 apps are accessed from the brightly-colored tiles on the Start screen. Click or tap on a tile to open the relevant app:

The Windows 8.1 apps open with the Windows 8.1 interface, rather than the more traditional Windows interface used with previous versions of Windows. However, the older Windows apps still use this interface.

60

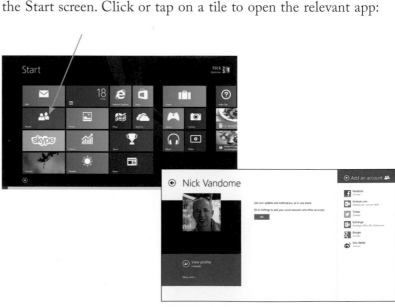

Windows apps

The Windows apps are generally the ones that appeared as default with previous versions of Windows and would have been accessed from the Start button. The Windows apps can be accessed from the Start screen by clicking on the **All apps** button at the bottom, left of the Start screen (see page 65 for more information). When Windows apps are opened from the Start screen they have the traditional Windows look and functionality. Windows apps open on the Desktop.

The **All apps** button can be accessed on a touchscreen device by swiping up from the bottom of the Start screen. It can also be accessed by pressing **WinKey** + **Z** on a keyboard.

Windows Store apps

The Windows Store apps are accessed and downloaded from the online Windows Store. Apps can be browsed and searched for in the Store and when they are downloaded they are added to the Start screen.

The Windows Store is accessed by clicking or tapping on the **Store** tile on the Start screen.

There are also new apps in Windows 8.1 for a Calculator, Alarms, Food & Drink and Health & Fitness.

See Chapter Nine for more information about working with Internet Explorer 11 in Windows 8.1 and Desktop mode.

See Chapter 10 for more information about working with the Calendar, Mail, People and Skype apps and how content can be shared between the different apps.

Windows 8.1 Apps

The Windows 8.1 apps that are accessed directly from the Start screen cover a range of communication, entertainment and information functions. The apps are:

 Calendar. This is a calendar which you can use to add appointments and important dates. It is closely integrated with the Mail, Messaging and People apps.

 Camera. This can be used to take photos directly onto your desktop, laptop or tablet computer, but only if it has an built-in camera attached.

 Desktop. Although this appears as an app on the Start screen, it takes you to the Desktop facility that has been available in previous versions of Windows.

 Finance. This is one of the information apps that provides real-time financial news. This is based on your location as entered when you installed Windows 8.1.

 Games. This can be used to play online Xbox games, either individually or by connecting to other online users and taking part in multi-player games.

 Internet Explorer. This is the Windows 8.1 version of the widely-used web browser. This version is IE 11 and the Windows 8.1 version has a different interface from the Desktop one.

 Mail. This is the online Mail facility. You can use it to connect to a selection of online Mail accounts (such as Outlook – previously Hotmail – and GMail).

 Maps. This provides online access to maps from around the world. It enables locations to be viewed in Road or Aerial view and can also show traffic issues.

 Music. This can be used to access the online Music Store where music can be previewed and downloaded. It can be also used to organize and play music.

 News. This is one of the information apps that provides real-time news information. This is based on your location as entered at installation.

...cont'd

People. This is the address book app for adding contacts. Your contacts from sites such as Facebook and Twitter can also be imported into the People app.

Photos. This can be used to view and organize your photos. You can also share and print photos directly from the Photos app.

Reading List. This can be used to save web pages for reading at a later time and even when you are offline. Items can be added by using the Share Charm.

SkyDrive. This is an online facility for storing and sharing content from your computer. This includes photos, documents and your Mail, Calendar and People information.

SkyDrive can also be used to share your content, such as photos and documents, with other people. See Chapter Eight for details.

Skype. Although this is not a built-in Windows 8.1 app it can be downloaded from the Windows Store and used as the default app for sending text messages and also voice calls to other Skype users.

Sport. This is one of the information apps that provides real-time sports news. This is based on your location as entered when you installed Windows 8.1.

Store. This provides access to the online Windows Store from where a range of other apps can be bought and downloaded to your computer.

Travel. This is one of the information apps that provide travel news and features. This is based on your location as entered when you first installed Windows 8.1.

The information for the Finance, News, Sports, Travel and Weather apps is provided by Bing.

Video. This can be used to access the online Video Store where videos can be previewed and downloaded. It can also be used to organize and play your videos.

Weather. This provides real-time weather forecasts for locations around the world. By default it will provide the nearest forecast to your location as entered when you installed Windows 8.1.

Using Windows 8.1 Apps

The appearance of the Windows 8.1 apps is different from those that have been provided with earlier versions of Windows. Their functionality is slightly different too in that the toolbars and settings are hidden and only appear when required.

Accessing toolbars
To access toolbars in Windows 8.1 apps:

1 Right-click anywhere on the **app**

2 The toolbar appears at the bottom of the screen. This is relevant to the individual app. Therefore, the toolbar will be different for the Photos and the Mail apps and so on

Accessing settings
Settings for individual Windows 8.1 apps can be accessed from the Settings Charm (the relevant app has to be the current one being used to view its settings):

1 Move the cursor over the bottom or top right-hand corner and click or tap on the **Settings Charm**

2 The settings options for the current app are displayed. Click or tap on each option to see the available settings

Don't forget

The bottom toolbar can be accessed on a touchscreen device by swiping up from the bottom, or down from the top, of the screen in the relevant app. It can also be accessed by pressing **WinKey** + **Z** on a keyboard.

Beware

Always check at the top of the Settings panel to ensure that you have accessed the settings for the correct app.

Viewing All Apps

There is a lot more to Windows 8.1 than the default Windows 8.1 apps. Most of the system Windows apps that were available with previous versions of Windows are still there, just not initially visible on the Start screen. However, it only takes two clicks on the Start screen to view all of the apps on your computer.

1 Move the cursor anywhere on the **Start** screen

2 Click or tap on the **All apps** button in the bottom left-hand corner

3 All of the apps are displayed. Scroll to the right to view all of the available apps

4 Click or tap on an app to open it

On a touchscreen device, swipe up from the bottom, or down from the top, of the screen to view the **All apps** button.

Apps that are installed from a CD or DVD are automatically included on the Start screen, not just the All apps screen.

When you move away from the All apps screen the apps disappear from the Start screen. You have to access the **All apps** button each time you return to the Start screen and want to view the full range of apps.

Closing Windows 8.1 Apps

Because they have a different interface from traditional Windows apps, it is not always immediately obvious how to close a Windows 8.1 app. There are three ways in which this can be done:

Closing with the App Switcher sidebar

To close a Windows 8.1 app from the App Switcher sidebar:

1 Move the cursor over the top left-hand corner of the screen and drag down to view all of the currently-open Windows 8.1 apps (see Chapter Two, page 31)

2 Right-click on the app you want to close and click or tap on the **Close** button

Closing by dragging

To close a Windows 8.1 app by dragging it off the screen:

1 Move the cursor to the top of the screen until the pointer changes into a hand

2 Click, or tap, and hold at the top of the screen with the hand and drag down to the bottom of the screen

3 Release the mouse at the bottom of the screen and the app will disappear

Closing with the keyboard

To close a Windows 8.1 app by just using the keyboard:

1 With the current app active, press **Alt** + **F4**

Don't forget

Any apps that open on the Desktop can still be closed in the traditional way of clicking or tapping on the cross at the top right-hand corner of the app.

Searching for Apps

As you acquire more and more apps, it may become harder to find the ones you want. To help with this you can use the Search Charm to search over all of the apps on your computer. To do this:

1 Move the cursor over the top or bottom right-hand corner of the screen and select the **Search Charm**

2 Enter a word in the Search box and select **Apps** from the list below the Search box

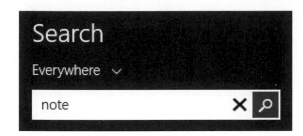

3 As you type, relevant apps are displayed. When the one you are seeking appears, click or tap on it to start the app

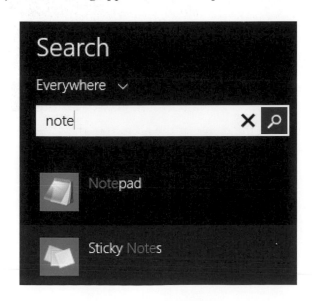

Hot tip

You just have to put in the first couple of letters of an app and Search will automatically suggest results based on this. The more that you type, the more specific the results become. Case does not matter when you are typing a search.

Pin to Start Screen

In most cases you will want to have quick access to a variety of apps on the Start screen, not just the new Windows 8.1 apps. It is possible to pin any app to the Start screen so that it is always readily available. To do this:

1 Access **All apps** (as shown on page 65)

2 Right-click on an app to select it, so that there is a tick showing in the top right-hand corner

3 When the app is selected, the bottom toolbar appears. Click or tap on the **Pin to Start** button

4 The app is pinned to the Start screen. It can now be repositioned, if required, as with any other app (see Chapter Two, page 33)

Pin to Taskbar

Since most of the Windows system apps open on the Desktop you may want to have quick access to them there. This can be done by pinning them to the Desktop Taskbar (the bar that appears along the bottom of the Desktop). To do this:

1 Access **All apps** (see page 65)

2 Right-click on an app to select it, so that there is a tick showing in the top right-hand corner

3 When the app is selected, the bottom toolbar appears. Click or tap on the **Pin to taskbar** button

4 Open apps on the Taskbar can also be pinned there by right-clicking on them and selecting **Pin this app to the Taskbar**

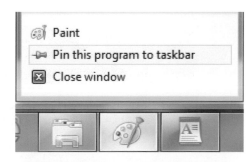

5 Pinned items remain on the Taskbar even once they have been closed

Hot tip

Apps can be unpinned from the Taskbar by right-clicking on them and selecting **Unpin this program from taskbar** from the contextual menu that appears.

Using the Windows Store

The third category of apps that can be used with Windows 8.1 are those that are downloaded from the Windows Store. These cover a wide range of topics and it is an excellent way to add functionality to Windows 8.1. To use the Windows Store:

1 Click or tap on the **Store** tile on the Start screen

2 The currently-featured apps are displayed on the Home screen

3 Scroll to the right to see additional featured apps

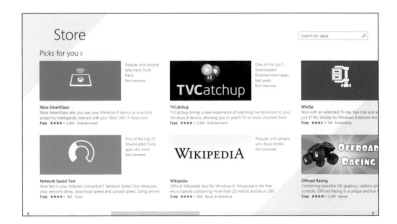

4 Select apps under specific headings, e.g. Top free apps

5 Click or tap on a category: the icons for the apps are displayed

6 Click or tap on a category and select an app to preview

7 Scroll to the right to view ratings and reviews about the app and also any additional descriptions

...cont'd

8 Right-click on the screen to view the top toolbar to view the available categories

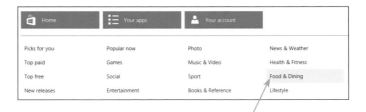

9 Click or tap on a category to access it

10 Click or tap on items in each category to view details about them. Click or tap on the Back arrow to go back up one level each time

Hot tip

To return to the Home screen at any point, right-click anywhere on the Store screen and click or tap on the green **Home** button from the top toolbar.

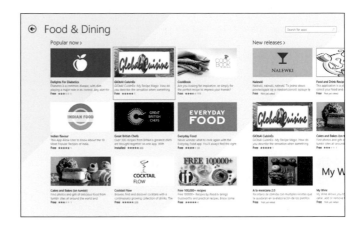

11 Enter a word or phrase into the search box to see matching apps. Click or tap on a result to view the app

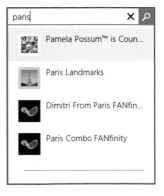

Buying Apps

When you find an app that you want to use you can download it to your computer or tablet. To do this:

1 Access the **Overview** screen for the app and click or tap on the **Install** button

2 The app downloads from the Windows Store, indicated by the Install button turning gray

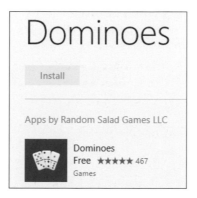

3 The app is added to the All Apps page and has a New tag next to it. This disappears once the app has been opened

4 Click or tap on the app to open it and use it

If there is a fee for an app, this will be displayed on, or next to, the **Install** button.

Once apps have been downloaded they can be reorganized and moved into different groups on the Start screen, or dragged away from their default group to start a new one.

Viewing Your Apps

As you download more and more apps from the Windows Store you may lose track of which ones you have obtained and when. To help with this, you can review all of the apps you have downloaded, from within the Windows Store. To do this:

1 Open the Windows Store and right-click anywhere on the **Home** screen

2 Click or tap on the **Your apps** link on the toolbar at the top of the screen

3 All of the apps you have downloaded are displayed, even if some have subsequently been uninstalled

4 Right-click or tap on an app to select it

5 Use the buttons at the bottom of the screen to, from left to right, clear a selection or install the selected app, if you have previously deleted it

Hot tip

When there are updates for apps that you have downloaded from the Windows Store, this will be indicated in the Your apps area.

Don't forget

You can reinstall apps from the Your apps section, even if you have previously uninstalled them. If there was a fee for an app you will not have to pay again to reinstall it.

74

Using Live Tiles

Before any of the Windows 8.1 apps have been used, they are depicted on the Start screen with tiles of solid color. However, once you open an app it activates the Live Tile feature (if it is supported by that app). This enables the tile to display real-time information from the app, even when it is not the app currently being used. This means that you can view information from your apps, directly from the Start screen. To use Live Tiles:

1 Right-click on a tile to select it. If it has Live Tile functionality, click or tap on the **Turn live tile on** button to activate this feature

2 Live Tiles display real-time text and images from the selected apps. These are updated when there is new information available via the app

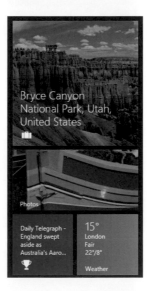

3 To turn off a Live Tile, right-click on a tile to select it and click or tap on the **Turn live tile off** button

Don't forget

The apps with Live Tile functionality include Mail, People, Messaging, Calendar, Photos, Music, News, Sport, Travel and Finance. Some of these, such as Mail and Messaging, require you to first set up an account before Live Tiles can be fully activated.

Beware

If you have too many Live Tiles activated at the same time it can become distracting and annoying, with a lot of movement on the Start screen.

Apps on the Desktop

The Windows system apps open on the Desktop, in the same way as with previous versions of Windows, even though they are opened from the Start screen.

Opening a Windows system app

To open a Windows system app:

Windows system apps here refers to any apps that are not part of the Windows 8.1 interface. Within this group there are some apps known specifically as Windows System apps too.

1 Right-click on the Start screen and click or tap on the **All apps** button

2 Select the app you want to open

WordPad

3 The app opens on the Desktop

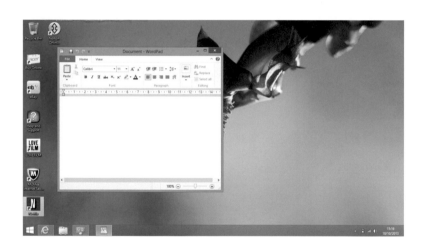

Hot tip

If apps have been pinned to the Taskbar, as shown on page 69, they can be opened directly from there by clicking or tapping on them.

4 Click or tap on the tabs at the top of the app to access relevant toolbars and menus

...cont'd

Closing a Windows system app

There are several ways to close a Windows system app:

 Click or tap on the red **Close** button in the top right of the window

2 Select **File > Exit** from the File menu

3 Press **Alt** + **F4**

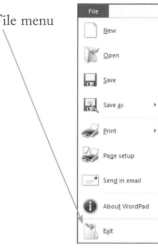

It is always worth saving a new document as soon as it is created. It should also be saved at regular intervals as you are working on it.

77

4 Right-click on the icon on the Taskbar and select **Close Window**

5 If any changes have been made to the document, you may receive a warning message advising you to save the associated file

Install and Uninstall

Installing apps from a CD or DVD

If the app you want to install is provided on a CD or DVD, you normally just insert the disc. The installation app starts up automatically and you can follow the instructions to select features and complete the installation.

Hot tip

You can access the Run function in Windows 8.1 by right-clicking on the **Start** button and selecting **Run** from the contextual menu.

Hot tip

Apps can also be installed from discs from the File Explorer. To do this, locate the Set-up. exe file and double-click or tap on it to start the installation process in the same way as in Step 2.

1 Insert the disc and click or tap on this window

> DVD RW Drive (D:) CS5 Design Prem1
> Tap to choose what happens with this disc.

2 Double-click or tap on the **Set-up.exe** file link to run it. Follow the onscreen prompts to install the app

DVD RW Drive (D:) CS5 Des...

Choose what to do with this disc.

Install or run program from your media

Run Set-up.exe
Published by Adobe Systems Incorporated

Other choices

Import pictures and videos
Dropbox

Open folder to view files
File Explorer

Take no action

3 Apps that are installed from a CD or DVD are added within the **All Apps** section

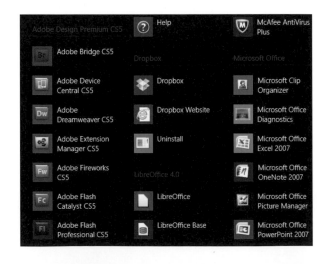

Uninstalling apps

In previous versions of Windows, apps were uninstalled through the Control Panel. However, in Windows 8.1 they can be uninstalled directly from the Start screen. To do this:

1 Right-click on an app to select it, as denoted by the tick in the top right-hand corner

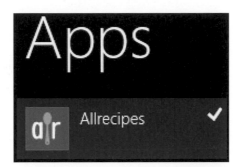

If apps have been installed from a CD or DVD they can also still be uninstalled from within the Control Panel. To do this, select the Programs options and click on the **Uninstall a Program** link. The installed apps will be displayed. Select one of the apps and click on the **Uninstall/Change** link.

2 Click or tap on the **Uninstall** button on the toolbar at the bottom of the screen

3 A window alerts you to the fact that related information will be removed if the app is uninstalled. Click or tap on the **Uninstall** button if you want to continue

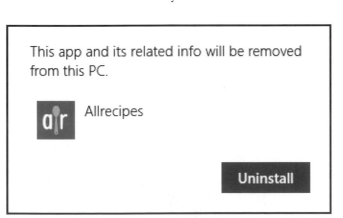

Some elements of Windows 8.1, such as the Control Panel, still refer to apps as programs, but they are the same thing.

4 If the app is a new Windows 8.1 one, or has been pinned to the Start screen, its tile will be removed from the Start screen. For other apps, they will no longer be available from the All apps option

Task Manager

Task Manager lists all the apps and processes running on your computer; you can monitor performance or close an app that is no longer responding.

To open the Task Manager:

1 Right-click in the bottom left-hand corner and select **Task Manager**, or press **Ctrl** + **Shift** + **Esc**

As an alternative, press **Ctrl** + **Alt** + **Delete** to display the Windows Security screen, from where you can start Task Manager.

2 When Task Manager opens, details of the currently-running apps are displayed

3 If an app is given the status of Not Responding and you cannot wait for Windows to fix things, select the app and click or tap on the **End task** button

If an app stops responding, Windows 8.1 will try to find the problem and fix it automatically. Using Task Manager to end the app may be quicker, but any unsaved data will be lost.

4 Click or tap on the **More details** button to view detailed information about the running apps. Select the **Processes** tab to show the system and the current user processes

5 The total CPU usage and the amount being used by each process are shown as (continually varying) percentages

...cont'd

6 Select **Performance** to see graphs of resource usage

7 The Performance panel shows graphs of the recent history of CPU and memory usage, along with other details

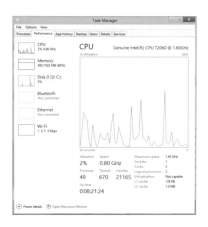

Resize the window so it does not take up too much space on your screen, and you can see the effects on CPU and memory as you use your system.

Alternative View

In addition to the standard view, with menus and tabs, Task Manager also has a CPU graph-only view.

1 To switch to the graph-only view double-click or tap the graph area on the Performance tab

2 To switch back to the view with menus and tabs, double-click or tap the graph area a second time

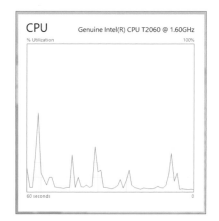

3 Select the **Wi-Fi** button in the Performance section to view the activity on your local area network. This tab also offers a graph-only view

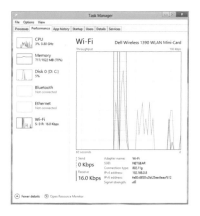

Don't forget

If you have a network adapter fitted to your computer, the Task Manager will feature a Networking tab.

Resource Monitor

The Resource Monitor provides an even more detailed view of the activities on your computer, and can be an essential aid in troubleshooting. To start the Resource Monitor:

1 From Task Manager, Performance tab Select the **Open Resource Monitor** button

Hot tip

Right-click any process and choose **Analyze Wait Chain...** to see which tasks are holding up an unresponsive application.

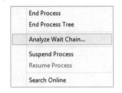

2 This displays CPU, Memory, Disk and Network details

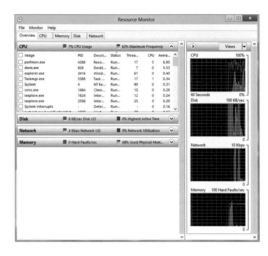

3 For even more detail, select one of the tabs, e.g. Memory

Don't forget

The Hardware Reserved section indicates how much of the 4GB maximum memory is unavailable to applications. With the 64-bit Windows 8.1, most of this memory would become accessible.

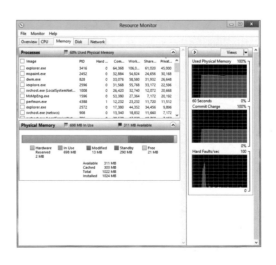

Ⓝ Open Resource Monitor

(4) Basic Controls

Even with the new Windows 8.1 interface, much of what you do will be with menus, dialog boxes and windows. This chapter shows how to use these structures on the Desktop and how you can control and manage working with folders and files.

Menus

Traditionally, windows have a Menu bar near the top, displaying the menu options relevant to that particular window. Some Menu bars consist of drop-down menus and others are in the format of the Scenic Ribbon.

Drop-down menus

For apps such as Notepad and Calculator, the Menu bar consists of drop-down menus:

 Open the app and click, or tap, on one of the Menu bar options to view its details

File	Edit	Format	View	Help
New				Ctrl+N
Open...				Ctrl+O
Save				Ctrl+S
Save As...				
Page Setup...				
Print...				Ctrl+P
Exit				

Scenic Ribbon

For Windows apps such as WordPad and Paint (and also File Explorer and Office apps) there is a Scenic Ribbon at the top of the window with the Menu bar options:

1 Open the app and select one of the Menu bar options on the Scenic Ribbon to view its details

Some options may have shortcut keys associated with them (e.g. **Alt** + **Up arrow** – Up one level), so you can use these instead of using your mouse. Other examples of shortcut keys are:

Ctrl + **A** – Select All   **Ctrl** + **C** – Copy   **Ctrl** + **V** – Paste
Ctrl + **X** – Cut   **Ctrl** + **Y** – Redo   **Ctrl** + **Z** – Undo

The Menu bar is not always displayed in folder windows. Press the **Alt** key to display it temporarily.

The ellipse (i.e. ...) indicates that if this option is selected, an associated window with further selections will be displayed.

If an option is grayed (dimmed out), it is not available for use at this particular time or is not appropriate.

Dialog Boxes

Although simple settings can be made quickly from menu options, other settings need to be made from windows displayed specifically for this purpose. These are called dialog boxes.

These examples are from the Folder Options dialog box. To access it, select **Options** on the View section of the Scenic Ribbon in File Manager and select **Change folder and search options**.

Tabs

Some dialog boxes are divided into two or more tabs (sets of options). Only one tab can be viewed at a time.

Check Boxes

Select as many as required. A tick indicates that the option is active. If you select it again it will be turned off. If an option is grayed, it is unavailable and you cannot select it.

You can select the option to **Always show menus**, and the menu bar will display permanently in folder windows.

Radio Buttons

Only one out of a group of radio buttons can be selected. If you select another radio button, the previously-selected one is automatically turned off.

Command Buttons

OK will save the settings selected and close the dialog box or window. **Cancel** will close, discarding any amended settings. **Apply** will save the settings selected so far but will not close, enabling you to make further changes.

Spin Boxes

Spin boxes let you type or select numbers only. They usually have arrow buttons to allow you to increase or decrease the values.

This spin box is from the Taskbar and Properties dialog box.

Structure of a Window

You can have a window containing icons for further selection or a window that displays a screen from an app. All these windows are similar in their structure. This example is for the File Manager.

Beware

Dialog boxes are usually fixed-size windows and therefore do not have scroll bars, minimize and maximize buttons or resize pointers.

Forward and Back

Address bar

Search box

Title bar area

Minimize, Maximize/ Restore Close

Scroll Up arrow

Command bar

Navigation pane

Slider

Scroll Down arrow

Scroll bars will only appear when there are items that cannot fit into the current size of the window. Here, only a vertical scroll bar is needed.

If you move the mouse pointer over any edge of a window, the pointer changes shape and becomes a double-headed resize pointer – drag it to change the size of a window (see page 89).

Double-click on an icon to open a window relating to it, in this case a WordPad application window. This window has a Quick Access toolbar, Menu bar, Scenic Ribbon, ruler, two scroll bars, and a Control icon at the top left.

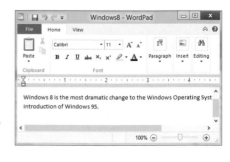

Moving a Window

As long as a window is not maximized, i.e. occupying the whole screen, you can move it. This is especially useful if you have several windows open and need to organize your desktop.

1 Move the mouse pointer over the Title bar of a window

You will see the whole window move, with the full contents displayed, and transparency still active, while you are dragging the window.

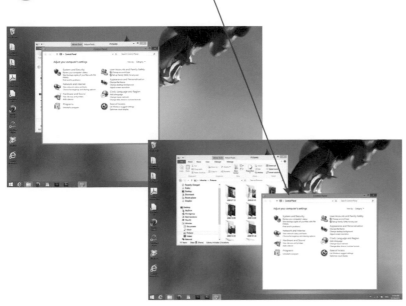

2 Drag the mouse pointer across the desktop (left-click and hold, or tap and hold as you move)

3 When the window reaches the desired location, release to relocate the window there

If you have two monitors attached to your system, you can extend your Desktop onto the second monitor and drag a window from one monitor onto the other.

Control Menu Move
There is a Move command for the window on the Control menu.

1 Right-click the Title bar and select **Move,** and the mouse pointer changes to a four-headed arrow

2 Click or tap on the window, holding down the left mouse button and moving the pointer towards the Title bar

3 The mouse pointer changes to an arrow, grabs the window and you can move and drop it as above

If the Title bar has a Control icon, left-click this to show the menu.

	Restore	
	Move	
	Size	
−	Minimize	
❏	Maximize	
x	Close	Alt+F4

Restoring a Window

You can also double-click, or tap, the **Title bar** to Maximize the window. Repeat the process to Restore it to the original.

You can also use Aero Snaps to maximize, move or resize windows (see page 92).

You can right-click the Title bar area or left-click the **Control** icon, to display the Control menu (see page 87).

Within the Desktop environment there are a number of actions that can be performed on the windows within it. A window can be maximized to fill the whole screen, minimized to a button on the Taskbar or restored to the original size.

Original size window   Maximize button   Maximized window

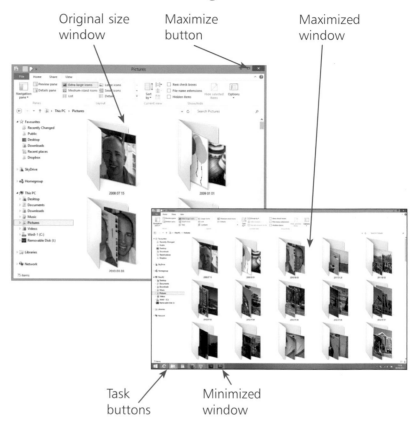

Task buttons   Minimized window

Whether a window is maximized or original size, click or tap on the **minimize** button (left of the top-right three buttons) to reduce the window to its Task button. This will create space on the Desktop for you to work in other windows. When you want to restore the reduced window, simply select its **Task** button.

The middle button is the maximize button or – if the window is already maximized – the button changes to the restore button.

Click or tap **Close,** the third button, when you want to close an app or to close a window.

Resizing a Window

If a window is not maximized or minimized, it can be resized.

Drag here
to resize
horizontally

Drag here
to resize
diagonally

Drag here to resize vertically

Resize and move all of the windows on your Desktop to organize the layout to the way you prefer to work, or see page 90 for other ways of arranging windows.

1 Place the mouse arrow anywhere on the edge of a window or on any of the corners. The pointer will change to a double-headed resize pointer

2 Click, or tap, and drag the pointer outwards to increase the size of the window, or inwards to reduce the size

Control Menu Size

There is a Size command on the Control menu which makes it easier to grab the edge of the window.

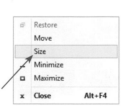

	Restore	
	Move	
	Size	
	Minimize	
▫	Maximize	
x	Close	Alt+F4

1 Right-click the Title bar (or left-click the Control icon) and select **Size**

2 The mouse pointer changes to a four headed arrow

3 Click the window, holding down the left mouse button, and move the pointer towards an edge or a corner of the window

4 The mouse pointer changes to a double-headed arrow and grabs the edge or corner, so you can stretch the window to the desired size, then release

Some windows are fixed and cannot be resized. These include dialog boxes and applications, such as the Windows Calculator.

Arranging Windows

If you have several windows open on your desktop and you want to automatically rearrange them neatly, rather than resize and move each one individually, use the Cascade or Tile options.

1 Right-click a clear area on the Taskbar to display a shortcut menu and select one of the arrangement options

2 **Cascade windows** overlaps all open windows, revealing the title bar areas and resizing the windows equally

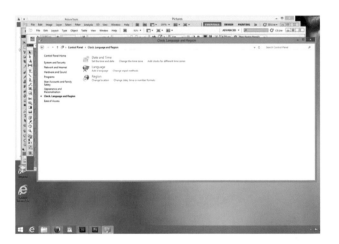

3 **Show windows stacked** resizes windows equally and displays them across the screen in rows

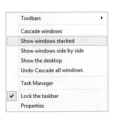

4 **Show windows side by side** resizes windows equally and displays them across the screen in columns

Beware

Only open windows are arranged, not minimized windows. Also, fixed-size windows such as dialog boxes and the Calculator app will get a proportional share of the screen, but they will not be resized.

90

Don't forget

When you right-click the Taskbar, all windows are deselected, so you must click, or tap, a window to select it and make it currently active.

Hot tip

When you have used a function to arrange windows, a matching Undo function is added to the Taskbar menu.

...cont'd

When you have a number of windows open on the Desktop, you might wish to see what is hidden underneath. For this, Windows 8.1 offers the Aero Peek function.

The **Show Desktop** button is on the far right of the Taskbar, next to the notification area.

1 Move the mouse pointer over the **Show Desktop** area, and open windows are replaced by outlines

This reveals the desktop icons. To actually select any of these items:

2 Select the **Show Desktop** area, and all the open windows are minimized. Repeat to redisplay the open windows

This Taskbar menu option is available in all editions of Windows 8.1.

Note that you could instead right-click an empty part of the Taskbar and select the option to **Show the desktop** (which then gets changed to Show open windows).

Aero Snaps

Aero Snaps provides a set of methods for resizing and moving windows around the Desktop.

Maximize Fully

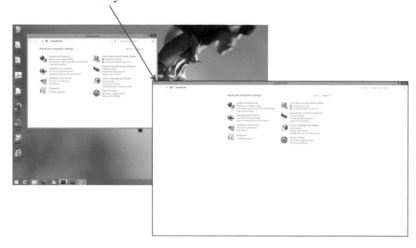

If the window you want to maximize is not the current one, click on it first, before carrying out the Maximize operation.

Click, or tap, and hold the Title bar and drag the window up the screen. As the mouse pointer reaches the top edge of the screen, the window maximizes. The shortcut is **WinKey** + **Up Arrow**.

Maximize Vertically

Don't forget

Alternatively, you can drag the bottom border of the window towards the bottom edge of the screen.

Click, or tap, and hold the top border of the window (until it turns into a double-headed arrow) and drag it towards the top edge of the screen. When the mouse pointer reaches the edge of the screen, the window will maximize in the vertical direction only. The shortcut is **WinKey** + **Shift** + **Up Arrow**.

Snap to the Left

To position the window to fill the left-hand side of the screen, click, or tap, the Title bar and drag it to the left. As the mouse pointer reaches the left edge, the window resizes to fill half of the screen. The shortcut is **WinKey** + **Left Arrow**.

Snap to the Right

To position the window to fill the right-hand side of the screen, click, or tap, the Title bar and drag it to the right. As the mouse pointer reaches the right edge, the window resizes to fill half of the screen. The shortcut key is **WinKey** + **Right Arrow**.

Hot tip

Alternatively, make the two windows the only open (not minimized) windows, right-click the Taskbar, and then choose the option to **Show windows side-by-side**.

Compare Two Windows

Snap one of the windows to the left and the other window to the right.

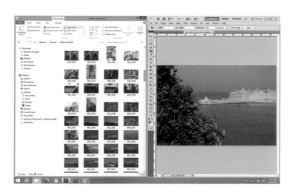

Restore

Drag the Title bar of a maximized or snapped window, away from the edge of the screen and the window will return to its previous size (though not the same position). The shortcut is **WinKey** + **Down Arrow**.

Hot tip

Double-clicking or tapping the Title bar will also reverse the maximize or snap. This restores size and position.

Switching Windows

If you have several windows open on your Desktop, one will be active. This will be the foremost window and it has its Title bar, Menu bar and outside window frame highlighted. If you have more than one window displayed on the Desktop, select anywhere inside a window that is not active to activate it and switch to it.

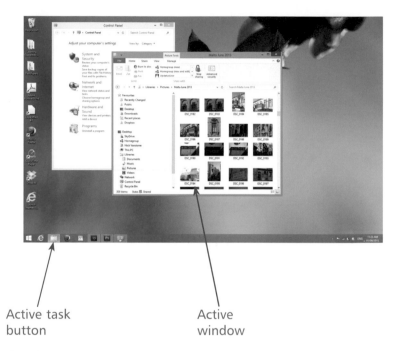

Active task button

Active window

Another method of switching windows is to use the Taskbar at the bottom. Every window that is open has a button created automatically on the Taskbar. Therefore, it does not matter if the window you want to switch to is overlaid with others and you cannot see it. Just select the button for it in the Taskbar and the window will be moved to the front and made active.

Move the mouse pointer over a task button, and a live preview is displayed (one for each window if there are multiple tasks).

Arranging Icons

You can rearrange the order of the items in your folders or on your Desktop in many different ways.

1 Right-click in a clear area (of the Desktop or folder window) to display a shortcut menu

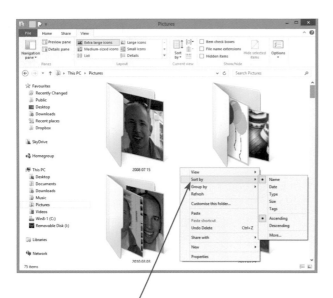

Hot tip

Select the **View** button to cycle through a range of views. Click, or tap, the **down arrow** to see the full set of options.

2 Move the pointer over **Sort by**, to reveal the submenu of sorting options and click, or tap, e.g. the **Name** option, to sort all the file icons in ascending name order

3 Select **Name** a second time and the files will be sorted in descending name order

Group By
You can select **Group by** for folder windows (but not for the Desktop). This groups your files and folders alphabetically by name, size, type, etc.

Closing a Window

When you have finished with a window you will need to close it. There are several ways of doing this – use the method that is easiest and the most appropriate at the time.

Open Window
If the top right corner of the window is visible on the Desktop:

1 Select the **Close** button on the Title bar

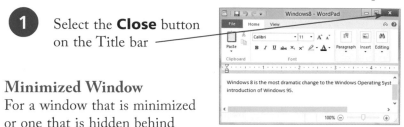

Minimized Window
For a window that is minimized or one that is hidden behind other windows:

1 Move the mouse pointer over the associated task button

2 Select the **Close** button on the Live Preview for the task

Control Menu
If only part of the window is visible on the Desktop:

1 Select the **Control** icon (top left corner) or right-click the Title bar

2 Select **Close** on the Control menu

Keyboard
To close any type of window use this key combination.

1 Select the window to make it the current, active window, then press **Alt** + **F4** to close the window

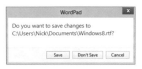

Don't forget

Save your work before closing any app window in which you have been working. However, Windows will prompt you if you forget.

96

Hot tip

Right-click the task button and select **Close** from the Jump List. If there are multiple tasks of the same type, the option offered is **Close all windows**.

☒ Close window

☒ Close all windows

5 Customizing Windows

The Desktop environment is still an important one in Windows 8.1 and this chapter looks at how to work with it and personalize it to your own requirements and preferences.

Personalize Your Desktop

As shown in Chapter Two there are plenty of
options for personalizing the Windows 8.1
Metro interface. There are also a variety of
options within the Desktop environment too.

1 Right-click the Desktop and select
Personalize, or

2 Open the Control Panel and select **Appearance and
Personalization** and then select **Change desktop
background** under the Personalization option

Add a personal touch
to your computer by
taking advantage of the
flexibility in Windows,
and personalize settings
associated with your user
account name.

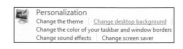

3 Select a new **Desktop background**. Click or tap here
to access additional options

The functions offered
depend on the edition
of Windows 8.1 you
have installed and the
hardware specifications
of your computer.

4 Click or tap on the Save changes button

5 The selected background is applied to the Desktop

Personalization options allow you to change Desktop background, color, sound effects and screen saver, either individually, or all four at once by selecting a theme.

Changing the theme

To change the overall theme of your Desktop, Taskbar and window borders:

1 Click or tap on the **Change the theme** link under the Personalization heading

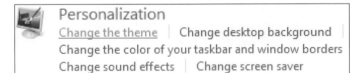

Personalization
Change the theme | Change desktop background
Change the color of your taskbar and window borders
Change sound effects | Change screen saver

Click **Browse** to select your picture folder then select an image as background or a number of images as a slide show. You can change the timing and randomize the sequence.

2 Select a theme in the same way as for selecting a Desktop background

3 Click or tap on this link on the themes page to obtain more from the Microsoft website

Get more themes online

Change Color and Sound

1 Open Personalization and click the **Window Color** button

2 The available colors are displayed. The default color is located in the top left-hand corner

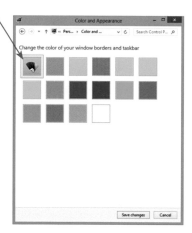

3 Select a new color, which is applied to all window borders and the Taskbar

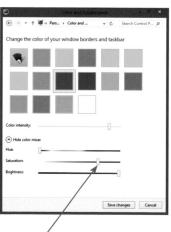

4 Drag these sliders to edit the selected color

1 Select **Sounds** from Personalization, to see the name of the sound theme that gets applied to events in Windows

Sounds
Windows Default

Click or tap the down-arrow on the Sound Scheme bar to try out a different scheme.

2 Select a Program Event and click or tap the **Test** button to hear the associated sound

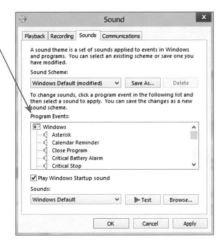

If you do not want to have sounds associated with Windows events, select **No Sounds**.

3 Browse to locate a new sound file (file type .wav), then select **Test** to preview the effect

4 Make any other changes, then select **Save As**, and provide a name for your modified sound scheme

Screen Saver

With the Screen Saver enabled, when your mouse or keyboard has been idle for a specified period of time, Windows 8.1 will display a moving image or pattern. To specify the image used:

1 From Personalization, select the **Screen Saver** button (which initially shows None)

Hot tip

The term Screen Saver derives from the days when a static image on the screen could get burned into the surface of the CRT. Although this is no longer a problem, Screen Savers are a useful way to lock up your system when you leave it unattended.

102

2 Select the **Screen Saver** bar and choose a screen saver, e.g. Bubbles

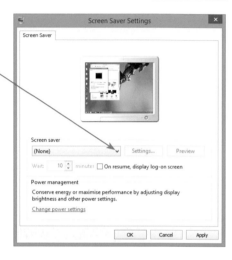

3 Select the **Preview** button to check out the action

4 Set the time delay after which the Screen Saver will be invoked, and choose to display the logon screen when the system resumes

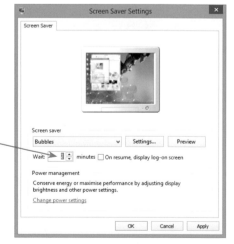

Don't forget

Moving the mouse or touching any key on the keyboard will cause the system to resume. It is usually best to tap the **Shift** key, to avoid inadvertently entering data or commands.

5 Click or tap **OK** to put the Screen Saver into effect

Personalization will now show the name of the Screen Saver that has been enabled.

Desktop Icons

To control the display of icons on the Desktop:

1 Right-click on the Desktop, click or tap **View** and select **Show desktop icons**. A check mark is added

2 To resize the icons, display the View menu as above and click **Large icons**, **Medium icons** or **Small icons**

3 To remove the check mark and hide all the icons, display the View menu and select **Show desktop icons** again

4 To choose which of the system icons appear, open Personalization and select **Change desktop icons**

Don't forget

You can use the scroll wheel on your mouse to resize desktop icons. On the Desktop, hold down **Ctrl** as you roll the wheel up or down.

5 Select or clear the boxes to show or hide icons as required

If you want to use the Snap function as shown in Chapter Two you need to have a minimum screen resolution of 1366 x 768.

Beware

If you have an LCD monitor or a laptop computer, you are recommended to stay with the native resolution, normally the highest.

Screen Resolution

If you have a high resolution screen, you may find that the text, as well as the icons, is too small. You can increase the effective size by reducing the screen resolution.

1. Right-click a clear section of Desktop and select **Screen resolution**

2. In the Control Panel, select **Appearance and Personalization** and select **Adjust screen resolution**

3. Click or tap the down arrow next to Resolution and drag the slider, then click or tap **Apply**

4. Click or tap the down arrow next to Orientation to switch the view to **Portrait**, e.g. for tablet PCs

Display Settings

1 Access the Control Panel and select **Appearance and Personalization** and then select **Display**

You can change your display settings and make it easier to read what is on the screen.

2 Select, for example, **Medium – 125%**, and select **Apply**

3 Log off so that the change can take effect, then log on

4 Everything on the screen is increased in size if the display size is increased

Ease of Access Center

1 Open **Appearance and Personalization** and select **Ease of Access Center**

Windows will read and scan the list of common tools. Press the **Spacebar** to select the currently-highlighted tool.

2 Click or tap on this bar to get recommendations on the settings that will be most appropriate for you

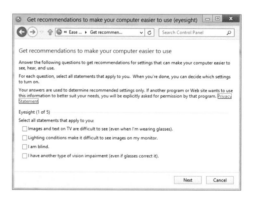

The Ease of Access Center allows you to turn on and set up apps and settings that make it easier to see your computer and use your mouse and keyboard.

3 Otherwise, scroll down to explore all the settings. Those you select are started automatically each time you log on

For example, to use the Magnifier:

 Start Magnifier

1 Open the Ease of Access Center and select **Start Magnifier** (or press the Spacebar while Start Magnifier is highlighted)

Hot tip

Move the mouse pointer over the Magnifying Glass and select it to display the Magnifier toolbar.

2 Select the **Views** button on the Magnifier toolbar to choose **Full screen**, **Lens** or **Docked** operation

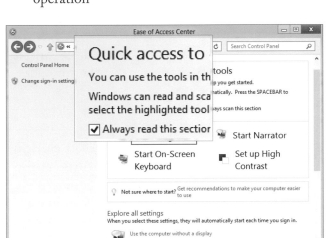

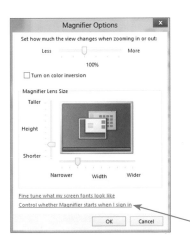
Don't forget

To stop using Magnifier during the session, right-click the Taskbar icon and select **Close Window**.

3 Select the **Options** button on the toolbar to specify the size of the Lens area, or to specify the tracking options for the other modes of operation

4 Select **Control whether Magnifier starts when I sign in**, to turn on Magnifier at start up

Date and Time Functions

To change the format Windows uses to display dates and times:

1 Access the Control Panel, and select **Clock, Language and Region**, and then the **Date and Time** option

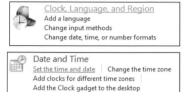

2 The current date and time is displayed here

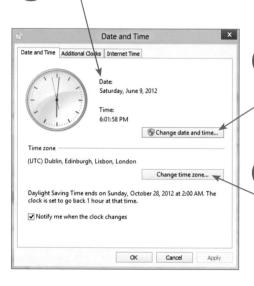

3 Click or tap on the **Change date and time** button to set new details

4 Click or tap on the **Change time zone** button to select a new time zone

Don't forget

When you select a different locale, the settings appropriate to that country or region will be applied.

5 Click or tap on the **Region** option in Step 1 and click on the **Format** tab. This can be used to determine the way that time and dates are displayed

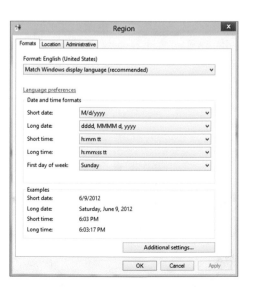

Hot tip

You can also review and change the way that currency and numbers (including measurement) are displayed.

108

6 File Explorer

The File Explorer is at the heart of working with the files on your computer and you can use it to browse all of the information on your computer and on the local network. This chapter shows how you can use the Scenic Ribbon function, modify the views in File Explorer, sort the contents and customize the style and appearance.

Opening File Explorer

Although File Explorer (formerly called Windows Explorer) is not necessarily one of the first apps that you will use with Windows 8.1 (those from the Windows 8.1 Metro interface are more likely to be examined first) it still plays an important role in organizing your folders and files. To access File Explorer:

Beware

This PC displays files from different locations as a single collection, without actually moving any files.

1 Right-click on the **Start** screen and click or tap on the **All apps** button. Select the **File Explorer** button, or

2 From the Desktop, click or tap on this icon on the Taskbar, or

3 Press **WinKey** + **E**, and File Explorer opens with the **This PC** folder

4 When File Explorer is opened click or tap on the **This PC** link to view the top level items on your computer, including the main folders, your hard drive and any removable devices that are connected

Hot tip

You can right-click on the bottom left-hand corner of the screen and access File Explorer from here too.

110

The Taskbar

The Taskbar is permanently visible at the bottom of the screen when working in the Desktop environment. To illustrate the range of functions that it supports:

1 Open items are displayed on the Taskbar at the bottom of the window

2 Windows of the same type will be grouped under a task button or a File Explorer shortcut button if available

3 Move the mouse pointer over the File Explorer shortcut to see previews of the folder windows that File Explorer is managing

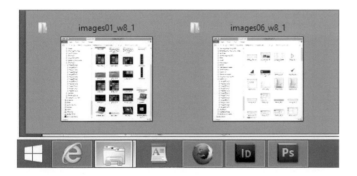

4 Move the mouse pointer over the other multiple Task button to see the customization and control windows, e.g. for the Control Panel here

111

Beware

In Windows 8.1 the Libraries are not visible by default. To show them, click or tap on the **Navigation pane** button and click or tap on the **Show libraries** button so that a tick appears.

Hot tip

You can also right-click the folder name in the Navigation pane folder list, to display the **New > Folder** menu.

Libraries

File Explorer can use the Library for accessing the files and folders on your computer and network. Each Library displays files from several locations. Initially there are four Libraries defined, showing files from the current user and the public folders:

● **Documents** – My Documents, Public Documents

● **Music** – My Music, Public Music

● **Pictures** – My Pictures, Public Pictures

● **Videos** – My Videos, Public Videos

To view the Pictures Library, for example:

1 Select **Pictures** in the Navigation pane

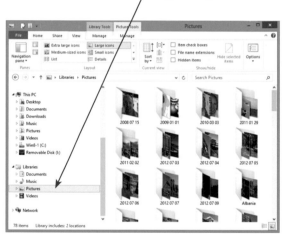

To add another folder to the Pictures Library:

1 Right-click in the Pictures Library window and select **New > Folder**

2 Click or tap on the folder name and overwrite it with a new title

Scenic Ribbon

The navigation and functionality in the Libraries is done by the Scenic Ribbon at the top of the window. This has options for the Library itself and also the type of content that is being viewed.

1 Click or tap on the tabs at the top of the Library window to view associated tools

2 Click or tap on the Library Tools tab to view the menus for the whole Library (see below)

3 Click or tap on the content tab (Picture Tools in this example) to view menus for the selected content

Library File Menu
This contains options for opening a new window, closing the current window or moving to a frequently-visited location in the Library.

Library Home Menu
This contains options for copying and pasting, moving, deleting and renaming selected items. You can also create new folders, view folder properties and select all items in a folder.

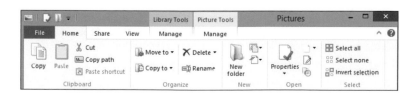

...cont'd

Library Share Menu

This contains options for sharing selected items, by sending them to the HomeGroup or another user on the computer, burning them to a CD or DVD, creating a compressed Zip file or sending the items to a printer.

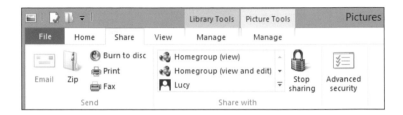

Library View Menu

This contains options for how you view the items in the current active folder (see page 122).

Library Manage Menu

This contains options for managing specific libraries. Click or tap on the Manage library button to add additional folders to the one currently being viewed.

Library Menu Options

If there is a down-pointing arrow next to an item on a Library menu click or tap on it to see additional options, such as the **Optimize library for** button, which optimizes the folder for specific types of content.

Hot tip

Click or tap on the **Options** button on the View Menu to set additional options for the operation of a folder and how items are displayed within it.

114

This PC Folder

The best way to look at the contents of your computer involves using the This PC folder. To open this:

1 Open File Explorer and select **This PC** in the Navigation pane

Navigation pane   Location   Search box

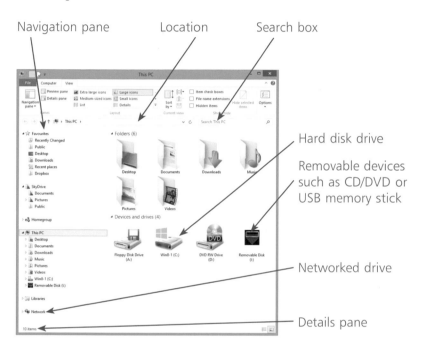

Hard disk drive

Removable devices such as CD/DVD or USB memory stick

Networked drive

Details pane

The Navigation pane provides the facilities you require to move between folders and drives.

2 Select items and double-click or tap to view their contents

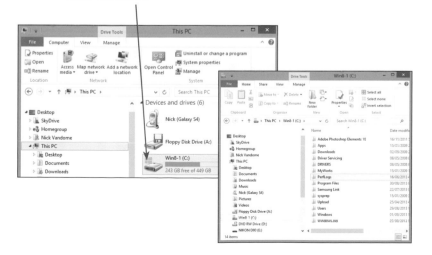

Exploring Drives

Explore the contents of any drive from the This PC Folder.

1 Select one of the drive icons – for example, the **Pen Drive** removable storage device

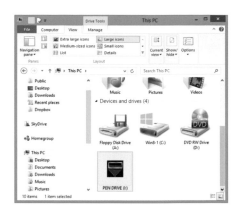

2 Double-click or tap the **Pen Drive** device icon (or select it and press **Enter**) to display the files and folders that it contains

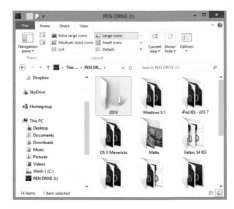

3 Double-click or tap a folder entry (e.g. 2013) and select one of the files that it contains

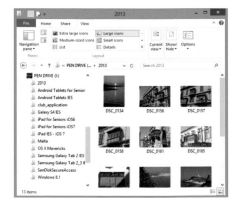

4 Double-click or tap the file icon and press **Enter** to open the file using the associated application, e.g. Paint

Don't forget

Press the Back arrow to return to the previous folder. See page 118 for more ways to navigate using the Address bar.

...cont'd

You can see all the folder entries in This PC in a structured list.

1 Double-click or tap the **This PC** entry in the Navigation pane

2 The Computer folder is displayed, and the fixed drives plus any removable drives with media inserted are listed

3 Select the ▷ open triangle next to a heading level, to expand that entry to the next level

4 Select the ◢ filled triangle to collapse the entries to that heading level

You can also explore the folders in your Favorites, Libraries, HomeGroup and Network of attached computers.

Resize the Navigation pane horizontally using the stretch arrow, and traverse folder lists using the vertical scroll bar.

Address Bar

The Address bar at the top of File Explorer displays the current location as a set of names separated by arrows, and offers another way to navigate between libraries and locations.

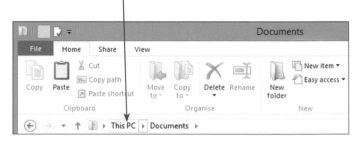

1 To go to a location that is named in the address, click or tap on that name in the Address bar, e.g. Documents

2 To select a subfolder of a library or location named in the Address bar, click or tap on the arrow to the right

3 Click or tap one of the entries to open it in place of the current location

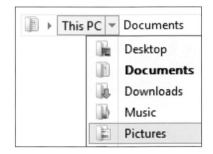

When you are viewing a drive rather than a library, the Address bar shows the drive and its folders, and allows you to navigate amongst these.

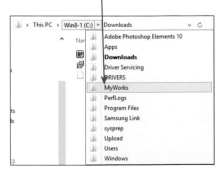

...cont'd

You can specify a new location using the Address bar:

1 Click or tap on the Address bar, in the space to the right of the set of names and the full path is displayed

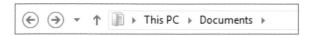

2 Type the complete folder path, e.g. **C:\Users\Public** (or click in the path and amend the values) then press **Enter**

3 The specified location will be displayed

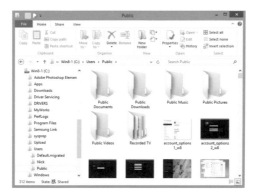

If you want a common location such as Desktop, just type the name alone and press **Enter**, and the location will be displayed:

The path is highlighted, so typing a new path will completely replace the original values.

You can switch to exploring the Internet, by typing a web page address. Internet Explorer will be launched in a separate window.

Navigation Panes

The normal view for File Explorer includes the Navigation pane. There is also a Preview pane and a Details pane available.

You can choose different panes to display:

1 Open File Explorer and click or tap on the **View** button. This will open the Scenic Ribbon

2 The Pane options are located at the left-hand side of the Scenic Ribbon

3 Click or tap on the **Navigation pane** button to view this format. This appears down the left-hand side

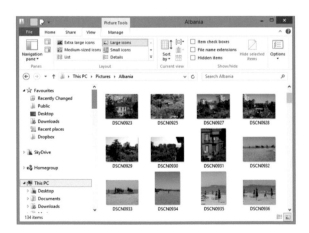

Beware

If you check **Off** the Navigation pane in Step 4, the left-hand panel will not be visible in File Explorer.

4 Click or tap on the arrow on the **Navigation pane** button and click or tap here to show or hide the Navigation pane. There are also options here for showing or hiding the Library and Favorites

...cont'd

5 Click or tap on the **Preview pane** button to view a preview of the folder or file selected in the main window

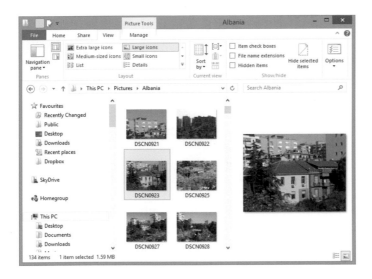

The Preview pane is particularly useful if you are working in the Pictures library.

6 Click or tap on the **Details pane** button to view additional information about the folder or file selected in the main window

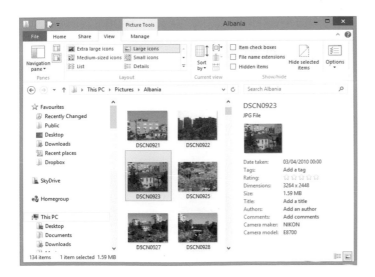

Changing Views

You can change the size and appearance of the file and folder icons in your folders, using the View tab on the Scenic Ribbon.

1 Open the folder you would like to change and click or tap on the **View** tab on the Scenic Ribbon. Select one of the options for viewing content in the folder

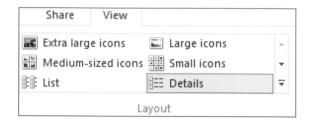

Don't forget

The way items are displayed within folders can also be set within the Folder Options (see page 126).

2 Click or tap on different items to change the appearance of icons

3 Pause at any position, holding the mouse button, to see the effect. Release the mouse button to apply that view

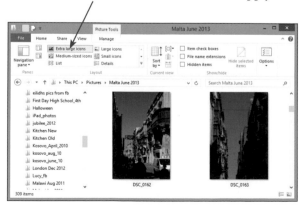

Sorting

Windows 8.1 allows you to sort your files in the drive or folder by various attributes or descriptors.

1 Open the folder, select **Details view** and select the attribute header that you want to sort by, e.g. Date

2 The entries are sorted into ascending order by the selected attribute. The header is shaded and a sort symbol ⌃ added

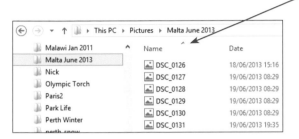

3 Select the header again, the order is reversed and the header now shows an inverted sort symbol ⌄

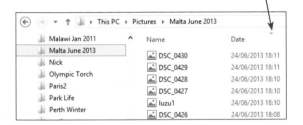

Hot tip

123

Note that any subfolders within your folder will be sorted to the end of the list, when you reverse the sequence. Libraries are an exception, and keep folders at the front (in the appropriate sort order).

4 The contents will remain sorted in the selected sequence, even if you switch to a different folder view

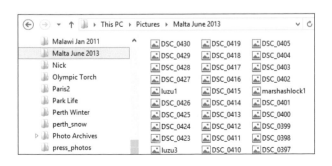

Filtering

Hot tip

This shows ranges of values appropriate to the particular attribute and based on the actual contents of the folder. These ranges are used for filtering and for grouping the items in the folder.

1 In the Details view, select any header and click or tap the **Down arrow**

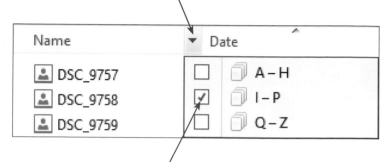

2 Select a box next to one or more ranges, and the items displayed are immediately restricted to that selection

3 You can select a second header, Size for example, to apply additional filtering to the items displayed

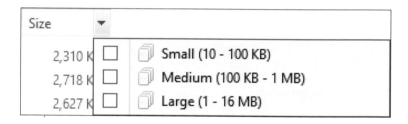

Hot tip

Filtering can only be applied in the Details folder view.

4 The tick ✓ symbol on headers indicates that filtering is in effect, and the Address bar shows the attributes

Beware

If you navigate away from the folder or close File Explorer, the next time you visit the folder, the filtering will have been removed.

5 Filtering remains in effect even if you change folder views, within the selected folder

Grouping

You can group the contents of the folder using the header ranges.
You do not need to select the Details view.

1 Right-click an empty part of the folder area, move over
Group by, then select an attribute, e.g. **Type**

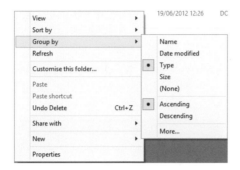

2 The contents will
be grouped, using
the ranges for the
attribute selected

3 Grouping is retained when you switch views (and when
you revisit the folder after closing File Explorer)

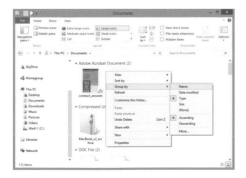

4 You can regroup the folder contents by selecting another
attribute. This will replace your original choice

The right-click menu
also offers the **Sort
By** option, so you can
specify or change the
sort sequence without
switching to Details view.

Any sorting that was
already in place will
remain in effect.
However, you can switch
between **Ascending**
and **Descending**.

Select **Group By,
(None)** to remove
grouping. Select
More... to add other
attributes. The new
attributes will also
appear in Details view.

Folder Options

You can change the appearance and the behavior of your folders by adjusting the folder settings.

1 From the View tab in the Scenic Ribbon, click or tap on the **Options** button and select the **Change folder and search options** link

2 Choose **Open each folder in its own window**, to keep multiple folders open at the same time

The same dialog box is displayed if you access the **Control Panel**, select **Appearance and Personalization**, then select **Folder** Options.

To open a subfolder in its own window, when the **Open in same window option** is set, right-click the subfolder and select **Open in new window**.

3 If you want items to open as they do on a web page, select **Single-click to open an item (point to select)**

4 Select the **View** tab to select options for how items appear in the File Explorer libraries

5 Select **Apply** to try out the selected changes without closing the Folder Options

Apply

6 Select **Restore Defaults** then **Apply,** to reset all options to their default values

7 Managing Files and Folders

Folders can contain other folders as well as files, and Windows 8.1 treats them in very much the same way. Hence, operations such as moving, copying , deleting and searching apply to files and to folders in a similar way. This chapter shows how to perform these tasks and actions while working with folders and files within the File Explorer.

Select Files and Folders

Single File or Folder

To process several files or folders, it is more efficient to select and process them as a group, rather than one by one.

1 Click or tap the item to highlight it, then move, copy or delete it as required

Sequential Files

Use the sorting, filtering and grouping options (see Chapter Six) to rearrange the files to make the selection easier.

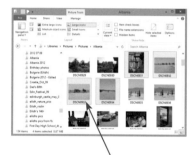

1 Click or tap to select the first item, press and hold **Shift**, then click or tap the last item, to highlight the range

Adjacent Block

You must start the box from an empty space in the folder. If you accidently click a file or folder, you will drag that item, rather than create a box.

1 Drag out a box to cover the files you want selected. All of the files in the rectangular area will be highlighted

...cont'd

Non-adjacent Files

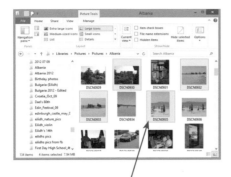

1 To select several, non-adjacent files, click or tap one item, press and hold **Ctrl**, then click or tap the subsequent items. As you select files, they are highlighted

Partial Sequence

You can combine these techniques to select part of a range.

1 Select a group of sequential files or an adjacent block of files (as described on the previous page)

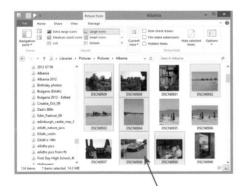

2 Hold down **Ctrl**, and click or tap to deselect any files in the range that you do not want and to select extra ones

All Files and Folders

To select all of the files (and folders) in the current folder, select the **Home** tab in the Scenic Ribbon and click or tap on **Select All** or press **Ctrl** + **A**.

To deselect one file, click it while the **Ctrl** key is being held down. To deselect all of the files, click once anywhere in the folder outside the selection area.

129

If you select a folder, you will also be selecting any files and folders that it may contain.

Copy or Move Files or Folders

You may wish to copy or move some files and folders to another folder on the same drive, or to another drive. There are several ways to achieve this.

Drag, Using the Right Mouse Button

For ease and simplicity, the prompted method, using the right mouse button, is recommended.

1 Open File Explorer and the folder with the required files, then locate the destination in the Folders list

2 In the folder contents, select the files and folders that you want to copy or move

This shows the number of files and the default action, e.g. **Move To** (for a folder on the same drive) or **Copy To** (for a different drive), but you can still choose the actual operation.

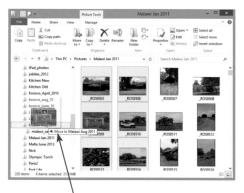

3 Right-click any one of the selection, drag the files onto the destination folder or drive in the Folders list, so it is highlighted and named, then release to display the menu

4 Click the **Move here** or **Copy here** option as desired, and the files will be added to the destination folder

Drag, Using the Left Mouse Button

In this case default actions are applied, with no intervening menu.

1 Select the files and folders to be moved or copied

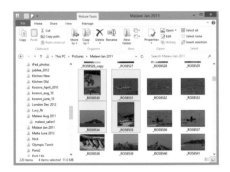

2 Use the left mouse button to drag the selection to the destination drive or folder in the Folders list, in this example the removable USB storage drive

3 Press **Shift** to Move instead of Copy to another drive. Press **Ctrl** to Copy instead of Move to a folder on the same drive as the source folder

In Summary

Drives	Drag	Drag+Shift	Drag+Ctrl
Same	Move	Move	Copy
Different	Copy	Move	Copy

Hot tip

Open File Explorer and the source folder, then locate the destination in the folder list, ready for moving or copying files and folders.

Hot tip

As you hover over a drive or folder in the Folders list, it expands to reveal the subfolders.

Don't forget

You will see a ✚ symbol if the file is going to be copied, or a ➜ if the file is going to be moved.

...cont'd

Using Cut, Copy, Paste

Hot tip

Cut does not remove the selection initially, it just dims it, until you Paste it (see step 5). Press **Esc** if you decide to cancel the move, and the item will remain in place.

Hot tip

Select **Send To**, to direct the selected files and folders to a device with removable storage, e.g. a USB drive.

1 Choose the files and folders you want to copy and right-click within the selection

2 From the shortcut menu click or tap **Copy** or **Cut** to move the selection

3 Right-click and click or tap **Open in new window**, for the folder in which you want to put the selection

4 Right-click a blank area of the destination folder

5 Select **Paste** from the menu to complete the Copy or move operation

Don't forget

When you Copy, you can Paste Shortcut (instead of Paste) to insert a link to the original file. However, this is inactive when you Cut files.

Keyboard Shortcuts

Cut, Copy and Paste options are also available as keyboard shortcuts. Select files and folders as above, but use these keys in place of the menu selections for Copy, Cut and Paste. There are also shortcuts to Undo an action or Redo an action.

Press this key	To do this
F1	Display Help
Ctrl+C	Copy the selected item
Ctrl+X	Cut the selected item
Ctrl+V	Paste the selected item
Ctrl+Z	Undo an action
Ctrl+Y	Redo an action

...cont'd

Burn to Disc

If your computer has a CD or DVD recorder, you can copy files to a writable disc. This is usually termed "burning".

1 Insert a writable CD or DVD disc into the recorder drive (DVD/CD RW). Click or tap on this popup

2 When the prompt appears, choose the option to **Burn files to disc** using File Explorer

3 Amend the suggested disc title if desired

4 Choose how you plan to use the disc you will be creating and click or tap on the **Next** button. The disc will then be formatted

5 Make sure the CD/DVD is selected and copy and paste files into the main window, or drag files there to copy them to the disc, or

6 Select files within another File Explorer window and click or tap on the **Burn to disc** button under the Share tab

Select the **Like a USB flash drive** option in Step 4 if you want to be able to use the files on another computer. Select the **With a CD/DVD player** option if you want to use them in this way.

You can use any of the methods described for copying or moving one, or more, files and folders (see pages 130-132).

133

File Conflicts

When you copy or move files from one folder to another, conflicts may arise. There may already be a file with the same name in the destination folder. To illustrate what may happen:

1 Open the **Documents > Windows 8.1** folder and the Pen Drive

2 Press **Ctrl** + **A** to select all of the files and drag them onto the Pen Drive, to initiate a copy of them

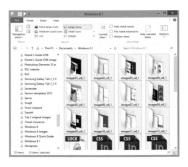

3 Windows observes a conflict – some files already exist, with identical size and date information. Select one of the options

4 If you select the **Let me decide for each file** option, details will be displayed so you can view if one is newer than another. Click or tap on the **Continue** button to perform additional actions on the file

Hot tip

You can, of course, use the Copy and Paste options from the right-click menus, or use the equivalent keyboard shortcuts, and File Explorer will continue to check for possible conflicts.

Open Files

You can open a file, using an associated app but without having first to explicitly start that app. There are several ways to do this:

Default Program

1 Double-click or tap the file icon

2 Right-click the file and select **Open** from the menu

3 Select the file, then click or tap **Open** from the Home section of the Scenic Ribbon. This will open the file in its default app

Alternative Program (App)

You may have several apps that can open a particular file type. To use a different app than the default to open the file:

1 Right-click the file icon and select **Open with**. Pick an app from the list or click **Choose default program** to set a new default app

2 The same choices are presented when you select the down arrow next to the **Open** button on the Scenic Ribbon in the folder window

When you delete files and folders from your hard disk drive, they are actually moved to a temporary storage area, the Recycle Bin (see next page).

You can press the **Delete** key on your keyboard, after selecting the files and folders, instead of using the menus.

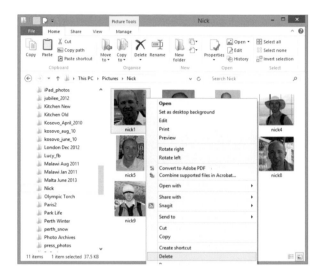

Delete Files and Folders

When you want to remove files or folders, you use the same delete procedures – whatever drive or device the items are stored on.

1 Choose one or more files and folders, selected as described previously (see page 128)

2 Right-click the selection and click **Delete**

3 Alternatively, click or tap on the **Delete** button on the Scenic Ribbon and click or tap on one of the options

If you choose to delete then immediately realize that you have made a mistake deleting one or more files, right-click the folder area and select **Undo Delete** or press **Ctrl** + **Z**, to reverse the last operation. For hard disk items, you are also able to retrieve deleted files from the Recycle Bin, and this could be a substantial time later.

You may need to have administrator authority to delete some files or folders from your system.

The Recycle Bin

The Recycle Bin is, in effect, a folder on your hard disk drive that holds deleted files and folders. They are not physically removed from your hard disk (unless you empty the Recycle Bin or delete specific items from within the Recycle Bin itself). They will remain there, until the Recycle Bin fills up, at which time the oldest deleted files may be finally removed.

The Recycle Bin, therefore, provides a safety net for files and folders you may delete by mistake and allows you to easily retrieve them, even at a later date.

Restoring Files

1 Double-click on the **Recycle Bin** icon from the Desktop or in the Navigation pane

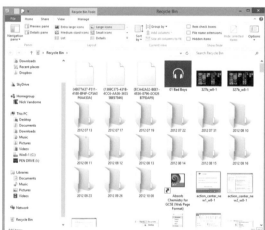
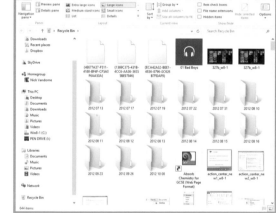

To see where the Recycle Bin is located, right-click the **Navigation pane** and select **Show all folders**.

	Expand to open folder
✔	Show all folders
	Show libraries

2 Select the **Restore all items** button, or select a file and the button changes to **Restore this item**

A restored folder will include all the files and subfolders that it held when it was originally deleted.

...cont'd

Permanently Erase Files

You may want to explicitly delete particular files, perhaps for reasons of privacy and confidentiality.

1 Open the Recycle Bin

2 Select the relevant files and folders, then select **Delete** from the one of the menus (or press the **Delete** key)

3 Select **Yes**, to confirm that you want to permanently delete these files (completely remove from the hard disk)

Empty the Recycle Bin

If desired, you can remove all of the contents of the Recycle Bin from the hard disk.

1 With the Recycle Bin open, select the **Empty Recycle Bin** button

2 Press **Yes** to confirm the permanent deletion

The Recycle Bin icon changes from full to empty, to illustrate the change.

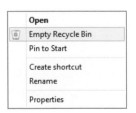

Bypass the Recycle Bin

If you want to prevent particular deleted files from being stored in the Recycle Bin:

1 Select the files and folders, right-click the selection but this time, hold down the **Shift** key as you select **Delete**

You could also just press the **Delete** key on the keyboard to delete items.

2 Confirm that you want to permanently delete the selected item or items. 'Permanent' means that no copy will be kept

Take extra care when selecting files and folders, if you are bypassing the Recycle Bin, since you will have no recovery options.

Deactivate (or Resize) the Recycle Bin

You can tell Windows to always bypass the Recycle Bin.

1 Right-click the Recycle Bin icon, then select **Properties** from the menu

2 Note the space available on Recycle Bin location (free space on hard disk)

3 Adjust the maximum size allowed, to resize the Recycle Bin

4 Click or tap the button labeled **Don't move files to the Recycle Bin. Remove files immediately when deleted**, to always bypass the Recycle Bin

This dialog box also allows you to suppress the warning message issued when you delete items.

139

Create a File or Folder

You can create a new folder in a drive, folder or on the Desktop.

1 Right-click an empty part of the folder window and select **New** and then **Folder**

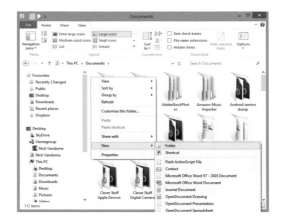

2 Overtype the default name New Folder, e.g. type *Articles*, and press **Enter**

To create a new file in a standard format for use with one of the apps installed on your computer.

1 Right-click an empty part of the folder, select **New**, and choose the specific file type, e.g. Text Document file

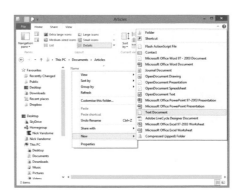

2 Overtype the file name provided and press **Enter**

Don't forget

Make sure that you click in the space between icons, away from the (usually hidden) boxes surrounding the icons.

Beware

If you click away from the icon without typing the new name, you get folders called New Folder, New Folder (2) and so on.

Don't forget

Normally, the file name extension (which shows the file type) will be hidden. To reveal file extensions, open **Folder Options**, select the **View** tab and clear the box labeled **Hide extensions for known file types**.

Rename a File or Folder

You can rename a file or folder at any time, by simply editing the current name.

1 Right-click the file/folder, then click **Rename**, or select the icon and click or tap on the icon name

2 Either way, the current name will be highlighted. Type a name to delete and replace the current name; or press the arrow keys to position the typing cursor and edit the existing name:

3 Press **Enter** or click or tap elsewhere to confirm the name

Preserving File Types

When you have file extensions revealed and you create or rename a file or folder, only the name itself, not the file type, will be highlighted. This avoids accidental changes of type.

Use the same method to rename icons on the Desktop. You can even rename the Recycle Bin.

You must always provide a non-blank file name, and you should avoid special characters such as quote marks, question marks and periods.

You can change the file type (extension), but you will be warned that this may make the file unusable.

Backtrack File Operations

If you accidentally delete, rename, copy or move the wrong file or folder, you can undo (reverse) the last operation and preceding operations, to get back to where you started. For example:

Hot tip

Undo mistakes as soon as possible since you would have to undo subsequent operations first. Also, only a limited amount of undo history is maintained.

Don't forget

The Undo command that is offered changes depending on which operation was being performed at the time.

Don't forget

If you go back too far, right-click the folder and select the available Redo operation, e.g. Redo Rename.

1 Right-click the folder area and select the **Undo Rename** command that is displayed

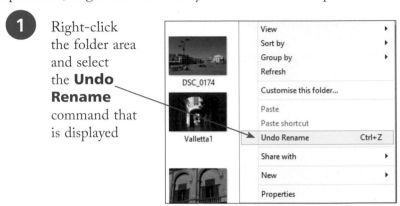

2 Right-click again, and this time there is an **Undo Delete** command for you to select

3 Now you will have reversed the last two operations, putting the folder and files back as they were before the changes

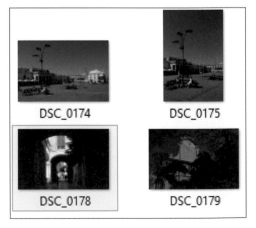

File Properties

Every file (and every folder) has information that can be displayed in the Properties dialog box. To display this:

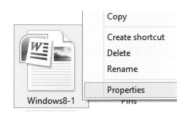

1 Right-click the file or folder icon to display the shortcut menu

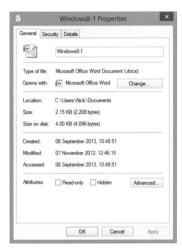

2 Select the **Properties** option, to display details for the file

3 Right-click a folder icon and select **Properties**, to display the folder information

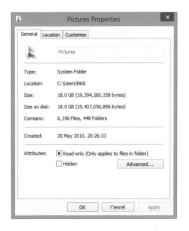

4 Similarly, you can display Properties for any of the Libraries

The purpose of the Properties dialog box is:
- to display details
- to change settings for the selected file or folder.

Click **Security** and other tabs, to display more information about the file or folder, and click the **Advanced** button for additional attributes.

In View mode on the Scenic Ribbon, select a folder and select the **Options** button. Then select the **Change folder and search options** link to view folder properties.

Search for Files and Folders

If you are not quite sure where exactly you stored a file, or what the full name is, the File Explorer Search box may be the answer.

1 Open a location, e.g. Documents, click or tap in the Search box and start typing a word from the file, e.g. *Nick*

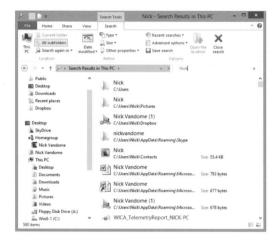

2 If that produces too many files, start typing another word that might help limit the number of matches, e.g. *Vandome*

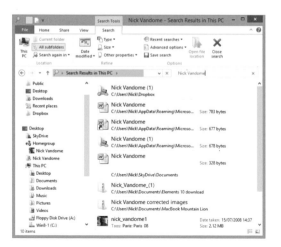

3 If the location is a drive rather than a library, its contents may not be indexed, so the search may take longer

Hot tip

Open the library or folder that is most likely to hold the file you want, and click in the Search box to initiate a search, looking at file names and content, limited to that folder and its subfolders.

Don't forget

Some files contain the search words in the file names, while others contain the words within the textual content.

Hot tip

For an attached hard drive, you may be offered the option to **Click to add to index**, and thereby speed up future searches.

Compressed Folders

This feature allows you to save disk space by compressing files and folders while allowing them to be treated as normal by Windows 8.1.

Create a Compressed Folder

1 Right-click an empty portion of the folder window and select **New > Compressed (zipped) Folder**

2 A compressed folder is created, with default name New Compressed (zipped) Folder.zip

3 Rename it (see page 141). You can also open, move, or delete it just like any folder

Add Files or Folders to a Compressed Folder

1 Drag files or folders onto a compressed folder and they will automatically be compressed and stored there

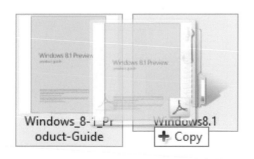

Hot tip

Compressed folders are distinguished from other folders by a zipper on the folder icon. They are compatible with other zip archive apps, such as Winzip.

Don't forget

To create a compressed folder and copy a file into it at the same time: right-click a file, select **Send To, Compressed (zipped) Folder**. The new compressed folder has the same file name, but with a file extension of .zip.

...cont'd

Compressed Item Properties

1 Double-click the compressed folder and select any file to see the actual size versus the compressed size

Right-click the file and select **Properties** to display this information, if the Details panel has not been enabled.

Extract Files and Folders

1 Open the compressed folder, drag files and folders onto a normal folder and they will be decompressed. The compressed version still remains in the compressed folder, unless you hold the **Shift** key as you drag (i.e. Move)

Extract All

1 To extract all of the files and folders from a compressed folder, right-click it and then click on **Extract All**

2 Accept or edit the target folder and click **Extract**. The files and folders are decompressed and transferred

If the folder specified does not exist, it will be created automatically.

Fonts Folder

Windows includes several hundred different fonts. These offer a wide range of distinctive and artistic effects in windows and documents, and support multiple languages and special symbols.

To view the fonts available on your system:

1 Access the Control Panel and open **Fonts** from **Appearance and Personalization**

2 The Fonts folder is displayed in File Explorer

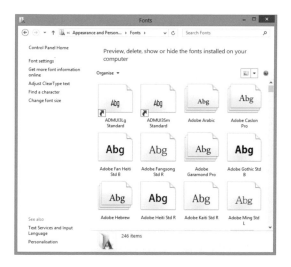

3 Double-click or tap on a group font such as Arial to see the font styles that it contains

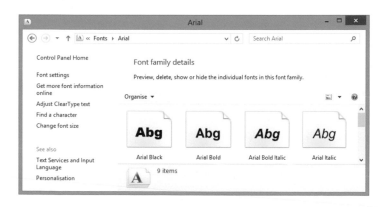

Don't forget

You can also find the Fonts folder within the C:\Windows folder.

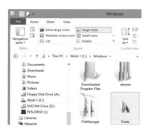

Hot tip

Double-click or tap on a font to see samples of the characters at various point sizes.

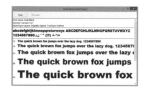

Character Map

As well as letters and numbers, the fonts contain many special characters, not all of which appear on your computer keyboard. You can insert these characters into your documents using the Character Map, or by pressing particular key combinations.

1 In the Fonts folder select **Find a character** to display the Character Map application

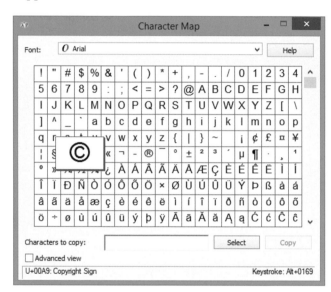

2 Select any character to see an enlarged version. The key combination and description is shown on the status bar

3 Click or tap **Select** to add the character to the copy box, and click or tap **Copy** to transfer it to the clipboard

4 Click or tap the Font box to select a different font from the list, for example Wingdings

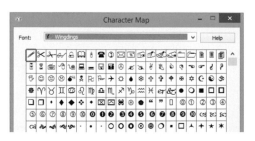

Select the Advanced View box to display more character set details and to show the Search box, where you locate a character by name.

(8) Digital Lifestyle

Windows 8.1 makes it easy to work with digital media with the new Photo, Music, Video and Games apps. This chapter shows how to work with these apps and also the SkyDrive function for saving your content online.

Using SkyDrive

Cloud computing is now a mainstream part of our online experience. This involves saving content to an online server connected to the service that you are using, i.e. through your Microsoft Account. You can then access this content from any computer, using your account login details, and also share it with other people by giving them access to your cloud service. It can also be used to back up your files, in case they are corrupted or damaged on your PC.

The cloud service with Windows 8.1 is known as SkyDrive and you can use it providing that you have a Microsoft Account.

SkyDrive settings can be managed by clicking or tapping on the **Settings** Charm and selecting **Change PC settings > SkyDrive**.

1   Click or tap on the **SkyDrive** tile on the Start screen

2   The SkyDrive folders are displayed

3   Click or tap on one of the folders to view its contents

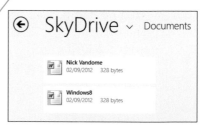

4   Right-click or drag up from the bottom of the screen to view the SkyDrive toolbar at the bottom of the screen. Click or tap on the **Add files** button to add files to the active folder

...cont'd

5 Click or tap on the **This PC** button at the top of the window and select **This PC.** Navigate to the files that you want to add to SkyDrive and click or tap on them to select them

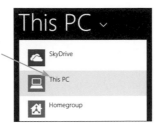

6 Click or tap on the **Copy to SkyDrive** button

7 The selected files are added to the active SkyDrive folder

When navigating for files, click or tap on the **Go up** button to go back up to the previous level in your file structure.

Using SkyDrive online

SkyDrive is an online service and this enables you to access and manage your files from any web browser with an active Internet connection. To do this:

1 Go to the website at **skydrive.live.com** and sign in with your Microsoft Account details

2 Your SkyDrive content is the same as in your SkyDrive folder on your computer. Click or tap on items to open and edit them

Click or tap on the **Upload** button to browse your computer for files to add to through the online SkyDrive site. These will also then be available through the SkyDrive app.

3 Click or tap on the **Create** button for options for creating new documents. These will also be available from your SkyDrive folder on your computer

Adding Files to SkyDrive

SkyDrive is built into the file structure of Windows 8.1 and as well as adding files from SkyDrive itself it is also possible to add them to the SkyDrive folder from your computer. Once this has been done the files can be accessed from SkyDrive from your computer, online or any compatible device, using your Microsoft Account login details.

Adding from File Explorer

To add files from File Explorer:

1   In the File Explorer, the SkyDrive folder is located underneath Desktop

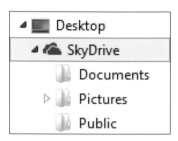

2   Click or tap on the SkyDrive folder to view its contents

3   Add files to the SkyDrive folder by dragging and dropping them from another folder or by using Copy and Paste

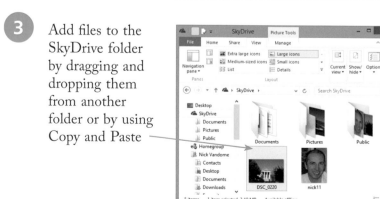

4 The new content is available from the SkyDrive app and also online from your SkyDrive account

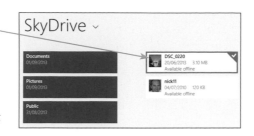

Saving files into SkyDrive
Saving files into SkyDrive

Files can also be saved directly into SkyDrive when they are created. To do this:

1 Open a new file in any app and create the required content

2 Select **File > Save** from the menu bar and select a SkyDrive folder into which you want to save the file

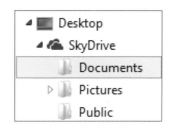

3 Click or tap on the **Save** button

4 The file is saved into the SkyDrive folder and will be available from the SkyDrive app and also online from your SkyDrive account

Hot tip

You can share your **Public** folder from your online SkyDrive account by opening it and clicking or tapping on the **Sharing** button. You can then email the link to the Public folder to selected recipients.

Don't forget

You can also share items from the SkyDrive app. To do this, right-click on an item to select it and click or tap on the **Share** Charm and select one of the options for sharing, such as with the Mail app.

Importing Photos

The Photos app makes it easy to transfer pictures from a camera, scanner, media card reader or pen drive. For each device, you connect it to your computer and then use the Import function in the Photos app. This is an example using a pen drive:

1 Plug the pen drive into a USB port on the computer

2 Click or tap on the **Photos** tile on the Start screen

3 Right-click on the Photos app Home screen and click or tap on the **Import** button on the toolbar at the bottom of the screen

Don't forget

The bottom toolbar can be accessed on a touchscreen device by swiping up from the bottom, or down from the top, of the screen. It can also be accessed by pressing **WinKey + Z** on a keyboard.

4 Click or tap on the device from which you want to import photos

Choose a device to import from

If you can't see your device listed, make sure it is connected to your PC, turned on and unlocked.

LEXAR (E:)

Select all · New folder · Import · Slideshow

5 By default, all available photos are selected, which is depicted by a tick in the top right-hand corner of each photo and a blue border

Hot tip

The Import function can also be used directly from within specific albums in the Photos app. However, the new photos are still imported into a new album.

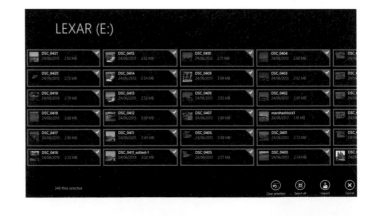

LEXAR (E:)

6 If you do not want to import all of the photos, click or tap on the **Clear selection** button

7 If you want to re-select all of the available photos, click or tap on the **Select all** button

8 If nothing is selected, right-click on individual photos to select them and click on the **Import** button again

9 The photos are imported into a folder named with the date of the import. Tap on the back button to go up to the main library where the folder will be displayed

10 Select a folder and accesss the bottom toolbar. Click or tap on the Rename button to change the name of a folder

Hot tip

To make a non-consecutive selection, right-click on the first photo then hold down the Ctrl key and right-click on all of the other photos you want to include in the selection.

Viewing Photos

Photos stored in your **Pictures** Library can be viewed with the Photos app. To do this:

1 Click or tap on the **Photos** tile on the Start screen

2 The available photo folders are displayed on the Photos Homepage

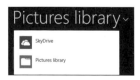
3 Right-click or swipe up from the bottom of the screen to view the Homepage buttons. This include options for selecting all folders and also creating a new folder within the Photos app or viewing your photos in a slideshow

4 Click or tap here on the **Details** button to view a list view of your photo albums

5 Details view contains colored tabs with the name of each album and the date on which it was created

2008 07 15 22/10/2012	2012 07 09 22/10/2012	eilidh_nature_pics 20/05/2010
2009 01 01 20/05/2010	Albania 20/05/2010	Eilidh_violin 20/05/2010
2010 03 03 22/10/2012	Albania 2012 05/11/2010	Eilidh's 14th 05/12/2010
2011 01 29 20/11/2011	Birthday photos 07/12/2011	eilidhs pics 05/06/2011
2011 02 02 20/11/2011	Bulgaria (Eilidh) 20/07/2012	eilidhs pics from fb 16/10/2011
2012 07 03 22/10/2012	Bulgaria 2012 - Edited 11/07/2012	First Day High School_4th year 08/09/2011
2012 07 04 22/10/2012	Croatia_Oct_09 20/05/2010	Halloween 20/05/2010

Pictures library⌄

6 Right-click or swipe up from the bottom of the screen and click or tap on the **Thumbnails** button to return to this view

7 Click or tap on an album to view the photos within it

⊙ Pictures library⌄   Malta June 2013

8 Click or tap on the back button at the top of the screen to move back up one level

⊙ Pictures library⌄   Malta June 2013

Don't forget

Move the cursor over the bottom of the screen to access the scroll bar for moving through albums and photos.

...cont'd

9 Click or tap on a photo to view it at full size

10 Move the cursor over the bottom right-hand corner and click or tap on these buttons to zoom in and out on the current photo

11 Move the cursor over a full size photo and click or tap on these buttons to move to the next and previous photos in the album

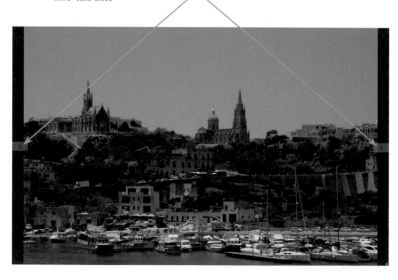

12 Right-click on a full size photo to access the bottom toolbar for the photo

13 The left-hand buttons can be used to, from left to right, delete the

photo, set a default app for which to open it, set it as the Lock screen or photo tile image or play the folder as a slide show

14 Click or tap on the photo and click or tap on the back arrow to move back up to the main album level

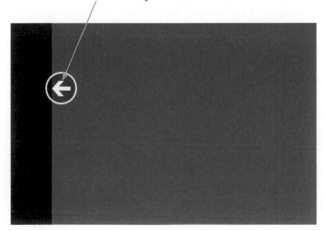

Don't forget

The buttons at the right-hand side of the toolbar can be used for editing the current photo (see the next two pages for details).

Editing Photos

In Windows 8.1 the Photos app now has a range of editing functions so that you can improve and enhance your photos. To use these:

1 Open a photo at full size and right-click on it or swipe up from the bottom of the screen

Select the Settings Charm and click or tap on the Options button to view the options for the Photos app.

2 The editing buttons are displayed at the right-hand side of the bottom toolbar. Use the **Rotate** button to rotate the photo by 90 degrees clockwise, for each click. Use the **Crop** button to emphasis the main subject by removing any unwanted background

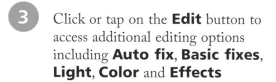

3 Click or tap on the **Edit** button to access additional editing options including **Auto fix**, **Basic fixes**, **Light**, **Color** and **Effects**

4 For the **Auto fix** option, click or tap on one of the thumbnails at the right-hand side of the screen to apply that effect to the photo

5 For the other editing options, click or tap on the required function to access the options at the right-hand side of the screen

161

6 For each option, click or tap on an editing button and drag on the enlarged circle to apply the effect

7 Right-click or swipe up from the bottom of the screen and click or tap on the **Undo** button to go back one step in the editing process

8 Right-click or swipe up from the bottom of the screen and click use these buttons to, from left to

right, save a copy of the edited photo, apply the changes to the original or cancel the editing changes

Playing Music

The Music app is used to access the Xbox Music Store. From there you can preview, buy and download music from the store and also listen to your own music that you have on your computer.

1 Click or tap on the **Music** tile on the Start screen

2 You have to sign in with a Microsoft Account to view the full features of the Xbox Music Store. Once you have done this you will be signed in automatically each time

3 Preview items are shown on the Home screen. Click or tap on the **Explore** button to view the full contents of the music store

4 Browse through the store with the categories in the main window. Click or tap on an item to preview it

5 Once you have selected an item, you can preview individual tracks, view information about the artist and buy albums or specific tracks

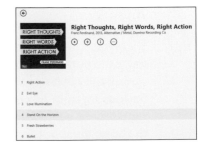

When you first log in to the Music Store, the Video Store, or the Games Store, you will be connected to the Xbox Live service.

Scroll left and right to view the rest of the available content.

Music that has been bought in the Music Store is then available to be played within the Collection section within the Music app.

...cont'd

Playing your own music

If you have music copied to your computer (see page 164) you can add this to the Music app and play it through this. To do this:

1 Access the Xbox Music Store through the Music app and click or tap on the **Collection** button

2 Click or tap on the **Choose where we look** link to find your own music

3 Click or tap on this button

4 Navigate to where your music is stored on your computer and select it so that it is available in the **Music** app

5 The tracks are added to the **Collection** section in the Music app. Click or tap on items, e.g. an album cover, to see the full

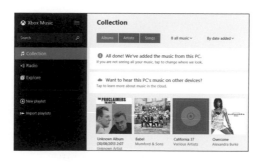

contents. Click or tap on individual tracks to play them

Hot tip

You can also add music that you have stored in your SkyDrive folder.

Hot tip

When playing music, access the bottom toolbar to use the playback controls. These include Shuffle, Repeat, Previous, Pause and Next. To do this, right-click or swipe up from the bottom of the screen.

Copying Music

As well as buying music from the Music Store, it is also possible to copy music from a CD onto your computer. This can be done through the Windows Media Player and once it has been copied it can then be added to your library in the Music app. To copy music with Windows Media Player:

1 Click or tap on the **Windows Media Player** app from the All apps section on the Start screen

2 Insert a CD, which will appear as a disc in the Library pane

Beware

Do not copy any music and use it for commercial purposes as this will infringe the copyright of the artist.

3 Right-click on the CD name and click or tap on the **Rip CD to library** link

4 The files are copied (ripped) from the CD to your Music library within Media Player

5 Click or tap on the Music heading in the Library pane to view the items that have been copied to Media Player

6 Click or tap on the Music library in File Explorer. The music that has been copied into Media Player is also available there and this is where it can be accessed by the Music app

Viewing Videos

For movie lovers, the Video app performs a similar purpose to the Music app. It connects to the Xbox Video Store from where you can preview and buy your favorite movies and TV shows.

1 Click or tap on the **Video** tile on the Start screen

2 You have to sign in with a Microsoft Account to view the full features of the Xbox Video Store. Once you have done this you will be signed in automatically each time

3 Preview items are shown on the Home screen. Scroll left and right to view more items

4 Scroll to the right and click or tap on the **Movies Store** link to view the full range of movies available

5 Click or tap on an item to see more information, view a preview clip and buy and download the movie

Beware

By default, DVDs cannot be played on Windows 8.1 computers. To do this you have to download and buy an enhanced version of the Windows Media Player from the Microsoft website.

Hot tip

If you download movies from the Xbox Video Store to your Xbox you can then use this to view them on your TV.

Don't forget

You can add your own video clips to the Videos app, from the Videos library in File Explorer, in the same way as adding your own music to the Music app.

Playing Games

The Games app can be used with the Xbox 360 games console. It can be used to play games, join friends for multi-player games, watch TV shows and movies and listen to music. It links into a number of services so that you can access content from websites such as YouTube and Netflix. To use the Games app:

1 Click or tap on the **Games** tile on the Start screen

2 You have to log in with your Microsoft Account details. Enter these and click or tap on the **Continue** button

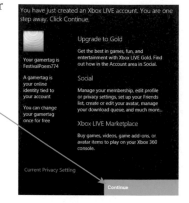

When you first log in to the Games app you will be given a gametag, which will be used to identify you on the Xbox games site.

3 Click or tap on a game to preview it and play it

You can also log in to the Xbox site at **www.xbox.com** to download games and find other people with whom to play games.

4 The Xbox website gives you access to a range of additional content

9 Internet Explorer 11

Internet Explorer, the widely-used Microsoft web browser, has been redesigned for Windows 8.1 and the latest version, IE 11, can be used with different interfaces whether it is in Windows 8.1 Metro mode or the traditional Desktop mode. This chapter looks at the difference between the two, introduces the features of the Metro version and shows how to use the Share, Search and Print Charms to transform your online web browsing experience.

Hot tip

Most ISPs also provide additional services such as email accounts, web servers and storage space on their Internet servers for you to create your own website.

Don't forget

It is usually better to use the software and procedures offered by your ISP, if possible, since they will be specifically tailored for the particular service.

Internet Connection

Before you can use the Internet and browse the Web, your computer needs to be set up for connection to the Internet. To do this you will require:

- An Internet Service Provider (ISP), to provide an account that gives you access to the Internet

- A transmission network – cable, telephone or wireless

- Some hardware to link into that transmission network

- For a broadband connection, such as Digital Subscriber Line (DSL) or cable, you need a DSL or Cable modem or router, usually provided by the ISP

- For dial-up connection, you need a dial-up modem, which is usually pre-installed on your computer

Your ISP may provide software to help you set up your hardware, configure your system and register your ISP account details. However, if you are required to install the connection or, if you are configuring a second connection as a backup, you can use the Set Up a Connection or Network wizard.

1 Access the **Control Panel** and select the **View network status and tasks** link, under the Network and Internet heading. This opens in the Network and Sharing Center

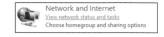

2 Click or tap on **Set up a new connection or network** link to display the connection options supported

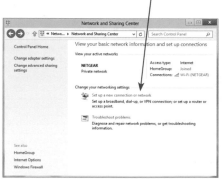

3 Select **Connect to the Internet** and click or tap **Next**

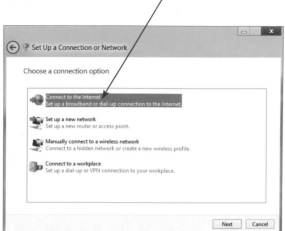

4 The Connect to the Internet wizard launches. Select the appropriate connection method from those offered

Windows identifies all of the possible connection methods based on the hardware configuration of your computer. If you have a wireless router or network, you may have an option for Wireless connection. If there is no dial-up modem installed, then the Dial-up connection method will not be offered.

Beware

If Windows has already recognized your connection, it detects this. You can select **Browse the Internet now** or **set up a second connection** (e.g. as a backup).

Don't forget

Continue through the wizard to complete the definition of your Internet connection, ready to start browsing the Internet.

IE 11 in Metro Mode

The default web browser, for connecting to the World Wide Web (WWW), provided with Windows 8.1 is Internet Explorer (IE) 11. However, there is a slight twist as it is a two-for-one browser in many respects: there is one version for the Windows 8.1 Metro interface and another Desktop version which will be more familiar to anyone who has used previous versions of IE.

IE 11 for Windows 8.1 Metro mode is optimized to display the maximum amount of screen estate, without a lot of clutter in terms of toolbars. It is also designed for touchscreen use, although you can use it perfectly well by using a mouse and keyboard too.

Don't forget

Every page on the web has a unique address, called a URL (Uniform Resource Locator) or simply a web address.

1 To open the Windows 8.1 Metro version of IE 11, click or tap on this tile on the Start screen

2 The IE 11 toolbars are hidden so that the web pages can be viewed with the whole screen

Hot tip

If IE 11 opens in Desktop mode rather than Metro mode, right-click on the top window border and click or tap on the **Menu bar** button. From here, click or tap on **Tools > Internet options** and click or tap on the **Programs** tab. Under **Open Internet Explorer**, make sure that the box next to **Open Internet Explorer tiles on the Desktop** is checked off.

3 Right-click on the screen, or swipe up from the bottom of the screen, to access

the Tab Switcher and the Navigation Bar at the bottom. Click or tap once on the screen or swipe downwards on the Tab Switcher to hide these items

...cont'd

Opening Pages

The Navigation Bar that can be accessed at the bottom of the screen (see previous page) can be used to open new web pages.

1 Type a web address in the Address Bar. When you click or tap in the Address Bar, icons of the pages that you have visited are available. Click or tap on one to open it

2 As you start typing a web address in the Address Bar, suggestions appear above it. These change as you add more letters in the Address Bar. Click or tap on one of the suggestions if you want to open that page

The types of website suffixes include: **com**, for commercial and businesses; **org**, for organizations and charities; **edu**, for education and academic; and **gov**, for government. There may also be a country suffix, for example: **com.au**, for Australia; **ca**, for Canada; and **co.uk**, for United Kingdom.

If you are entering a web address into IE 11 you do not require the initial 'www:'. As you start typing the address, suggestions will appear.

171

When you hover over a link in IE 11 in Metro mode, the link to the associated page is shown in a tooltip box at the bottom of the screen.

Hot tip

If you are viewing IE 11 in Metro mode on a touchscreen device you can zoom in on a web page by pinching outwards with two fingers. Pinch inwards to zoom out.

Navigating Pages

Because of the simplified interface for IE 11 in Metro mode there is not the same range of functionality of the Desktop version. However, this also means that pages can be navigated around quickly and efficiently with a few clicks or taps.

1 Use these buttons on the Navigation Bar at the bottom of the screen to, from left to right, refresh/stop the current page, view open tabs, add a page as a favorite and access page tools

2 When moving between different web pages, move the cursor over the left edge and click or tap on the **Back arrow**. Do the same at the opposite side of the screen for the **Forward** button

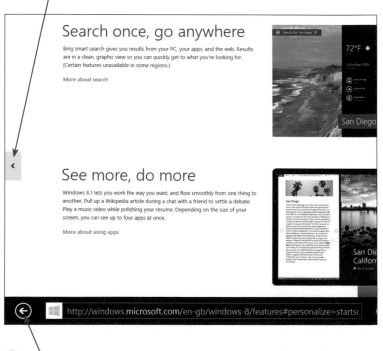

3 Click or tap on this button on the Address Bar for the Back function (the **Forward** button is on the other side)

Pinning a Web Page

If you have favorite web pages that you visit often it can be frustrating having to access them through IE 11 each time, even with the frequently-visited pages as shown on page 171. A solution to this is to pin a link to the Start screen. This means that you can access the page directly from the Start screen; IE 11 will be opened at the selected page. To pin a web page:

1 Open the required web page, right-click to access the Address Bar and click or tap on the **Favorites** button

2 Click or tap on the **Pin Site** button

3 Click or tap on the **Pin to Start** button.
(Enter the accompanying text if required. This will appear on the Start screen tile)

4 The link to the page is added to the Start screen as a new tile. Click or tap on this to open the page directly

Access the IE 11 Address Bar by right-clicking on a web page or swiping up from the bottom of the screen.

The **Favorites** button in Step 1 can also be used to add your favorite pages to the Favorites Bar in IE 11. These can then be accessed whenever the Favorites button is clicked or tapped.

Tabs in Metro Mode

Tabs within web browsers are now an established part of our online experience. This enables multiple web pages to be open in the same window. Each tab can have its own content displayed. In IE 11 in Metro mode, tabs are accommodated by the Tab Switcher that is accessed at the bottom of the screen by right-clicking on the main screen, or dragging up from the bottom of the screen on a touchscreen device. To work with tabs in IE 11 in Metro mode:

1 Click or tap on this button at the right-hand side of the Tab Switcher to add a new tab

2 Open a web page in the regular way

3 The open tabs are displayed on the Tab Switcher. Click or tap on a tab to access that page. Click or tap on the cross on the tab thumbnail to close a tab

4 Click or tap on this button to open an InPrivate Browsing tab or close all of the currently-open tabs

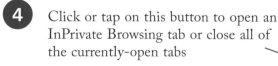

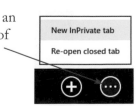

Click or tap on the **Tabs** button to view the open tabs on your computer and also any others that you are using with your Microsoft Account.

InPrivate browsing leaves no record of the browser session, in terms of pages visited. Therefore it is not a good option if children are using it.

IE 11 Metro Settings

As with other Windows 8.1 apps, IE 11 in Metro mode has its own settings which are accessed from the Settings Charm.

1 Open a web page in IE 11 Metro mode. Move the cursor over the bottom right-hand corner (or swipe from the side of the screen) and click or tap on the **Settings Charm**

Some tasks within IE 11 require add-on apps to perform them. When one of these tasks is undertaken, you will be prompted to download the relevant add-on.

2 Click or tap on the **Options** link

175

3 Options can be applied for always showing the Address Bar and Tab Switcher, increasing the magnification in IE 11, selecting a Homepage for when the browser opens, deleting the browsing history, and options for saving passwords when they are entered into websites

Other settings for IE 11 include Privacy, About, Help, Accounts and Permissions.

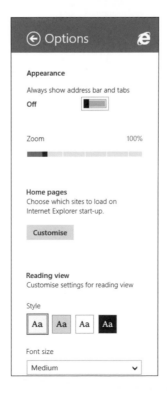

Sharing in IE 11

When it comes to sharing web pages with other people, the functionality of the Windows 8.1 interface really comes into its own. This is one area where the Charms can be used to connect and utilize other apps, including from IE 11. To do this:

1 Open the web page that you want to share and access the **Share Charm**

2 The Share options include opening the Mail and People apps to select people for sharing with and also the Reading List for saving the page for reading at a later time, even if you are offline and not connected to the Internet

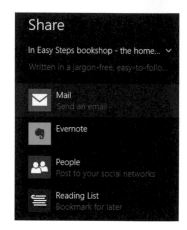

176

3 For the Mail option, an email is created, to which you can add a recipient. The email contains a link to the web page and a brief description of it

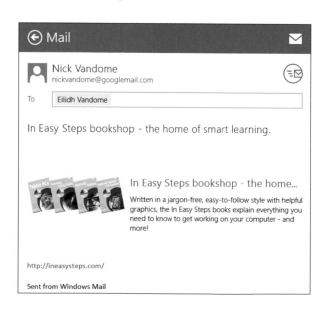

Printing in IE 11

The Charms can also be used to print active web pages.

1 Open the web page that you want to print and access the **Devices Charm**

2 Click or tap on the device you want to use

3 The web page is displayed in Print Preview

Many websites have a print version that is optimized for the printing process.

4 Select the number of prints and the orientation (Portrait or Landscape). Click or tap on the **More settings** link for additional print options

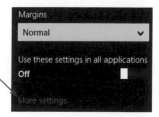

5 Click or tap on the **Print** button

Searching in IE 11

Searching for content is an integral part of using the Web. This can be done with a search engine on the Web itself, or the Search Charm can also be used within IE 11 in Metro mode.

1 Open IE 11 in Metro mode and click or tap on the **Search Charm**

2 Enter a search word or phrase

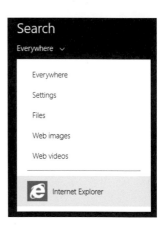

The default search in IE 11 using the Search Charm is performed by the Bing search engine.

178

3 Click or tap on the **Everywhere** button at the top of the search window and click or tap on the **Internet Explorer** button (if **Everywhere** is selected the search will be conducted across the Web and also your computer, which may be preferable in some cases)

4 The search results are displayed within the search window. Click or tap on one of the links to go to that page

Flip Ahead in IE 11

The Flip ahead function in IE 11 is one that facilitates the quick navigation between long pages of content that are linked together but appear as separate web pages. For instance, long documents that are traditionally linked with 'Read more' or 'Next page' links can now be viewed with Flip ahead. Results for web searches are another good option for this as it enables you to move quickly through multiple pages of results. To do this:

1 Access a web page with multiple linked pages, such as a search results page

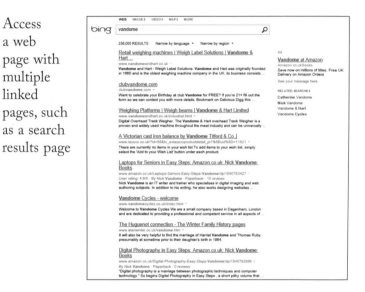

2 Move the cursor over the middle-right edge and click or tap on this button

3 The next linked page is accessed without the need to activate another link

IE 11 on the Desktop

IE 11 for the Desktop will have a more familiar look and feel to users of previous versions of IE and it also has a wider range of functionality. The main ways to access it are:

1 Access the Internet Explorer icon on the Taskbar

2 Within IE 11 in Metro mode, click or tap on the **Page Tools** button and click or tap on the **View on the desktop** link

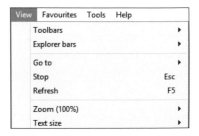

The Desktop version of IE 11 includes:

Menu bar   Address bar (with URL)   Tabbed browsing (multipage)   Favorites bar

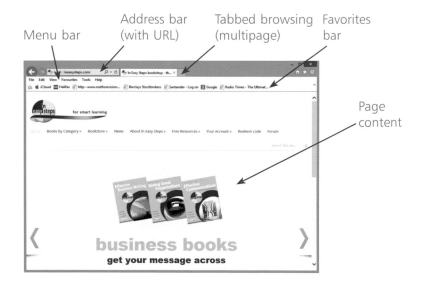

Page content

Menu Bar

At the top of the browser window is the Menu bar that contains sections with much of the functionality of IE 11. Click or tap on one of the headings to view the additional options. If there is an arrow next to an item it means that there are more options for this item.

Browser Controls

The Desktop version of IE 11 has considerable functionality:

Back and Forward
Select the **back** and **forward** buttons
to switch between recently-visited web
pages, or hold on one of the buttons to
select an entry from the Recent Pages list.

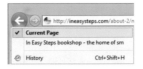

Tabs
Tabs allow you to view multiple web pages in
the same Internet Explorer window (see
page 186).

The Address Bar
This is where web addresses are
entered and includes access to

the Search box, a page compatibility view and the **Refresh** and
Stop buttons to control the loading of the web page specified in
the address box. This changes to the **Go To** button when a web
address is entered.

The Search Box
The Address Bar can also be used as a
Search Box. To do this, enter a word
in the Address Bar. In the results
window, click or tap on **Turn On
Suggestions**. The results will be
displayed as links to web pages and
search suggestions.

InPrivate Browsing is
a way of viewing web
pages without any of the
information being stored
by the browser. For
instance, it will not show
up in your browsing
history or store cookies.

Command Bar
This is accessed from
the **View > Toolbars**

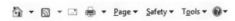

option on the Menu bar and contains items for setting the
Homepage, RSS feeds, reading emails, printing, page information
and safety items such as deleting browsing history and selecting
InPrivate Browsing, and web page tools.

Favorites Button and Favorites Center
The Favorites button displays the Favorites
Center, with the favorites, feeds and website
history (see page 182).

181

Bookmark Favorites

If you see a web page that you want to revisit, add it to your Favorites list to save having to record or remember the address.

1 While viewing the page, click or tap on the **Favorites** button

(see page 181) and then click or tap on the **Add to Favorites** button (or press **Ctrl + D**)

Open the Favorites Center as shown on the previous page and click on this button to pin it within the browser window so that it stays open.

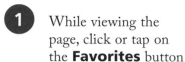

2 The page title is used as the name for the new favorite, but you can type an alternative name if you wish

3 Select **Add** to save the details in your Favorites list

View Favorites

1 Select the **Favorites Center** button and click or tap on the **Favorites** button (if not already selected)

You can also right-click any link in a web page or in search results, and select **Add to favorites**.

2 Click or tap on a folder name to expand it

3 Click or tap any Favorites entry to display that web page

4 Click or tap on **Add to favorites** and **Organize favorites**, to move, rename or delete the entries

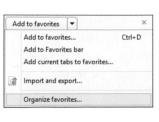

RSS Feeds

RSS (Really Simple Syndication) Feeds provide the frequently-updated content from a news or blog website. Internet Explorer can discover and display feeds as you visit websites, or you can subscribe to feeds to automatically check for and download updates that you can view later.

Discover a Feed

1 Open Internet Explorer and browse to a website that has feeds, for example the CNN website (**www.cnn.com**). The Feeds button changes color to let you know

2 Click or tap on the arrow next to the **Feeds** button to see the list of feeds available

3 Click or tap on one of the feeds to view the contents and you are offered the opportunity to subscribe, so that feed updates will be automatically downloaded

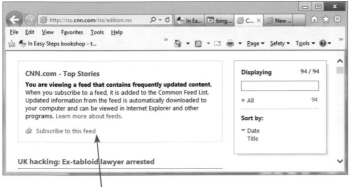

Don't forget

To view your subscribed feeds, select the **Favorites Center** button and then select the **Feeds** button.

4 Select **Subscribe to this feed**, then click or tap the **Subscribe** button, to add the feed to your list in the Favorites Center

oko. ok

OK

x

History

Hot tip

You can also press **Ctrl + H** to open the Favorites Center at the History section.

1 Open the Favorites Center and select the **History** tab

2 Pin the Favorites Center to the window (see page 182), so you can browse the History entries

3 Select the **down arrow** on the bar below the History tab, to change the sort order for the entries

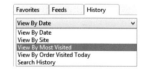

Manage the History

Don't forget

The general Internet Options also cover Homepage, Startup, Tabs and Appearance settings.

1 From the Menu bar select **Tools > Internet options** and select the **General** tab

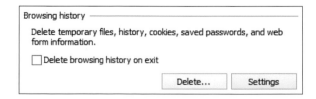

2 At Browsing history, select **Delete** to remove the records, or **Settings** to change the history period (default 20 days)

Homepage

Your Homepage is displayed when you start Internet Explorer or when you click the Home button. The web page displayed may be the Windows default, or may have been defined by your ISP or your computer supplier. However, you can choose any web page as your Homepage.

Current web page

1 With the preferred web page displayed, select the arrow next to the **Home** button on the Command bar and select **Add or change home page**

2 Select **Use this webpage as your only home page** or select another option

Reset Homepage

1 Select **Tools > Internet Options** and select the **General** tab

2 Select **Use default** to use the default Homepage specified by Internet Explorer

or

Select **Use new tab** to specify a Homepage for when a new tab is created

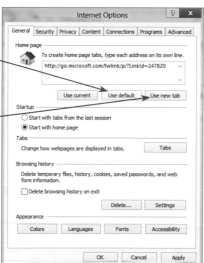

3 Click or tap **OK** to save the changes

Tabbed Browsing

You can open multiple websites in a single browser window, with each web page on a separate tab.

1 To open another tab, click or tap on the **New Tab** button

2 Type an address in the Address Bar and press **Enter** or click or tap on one of the frequently-visited sites

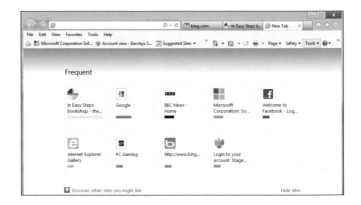

3 To switch between tabs, select the page tab on the tab row

4 Close IE 11 and you will be asked if you want to **Close all tabs** or just **Close current tab**

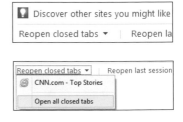

5 You can Reopen closed tabs from a new tab by clicking or tapping on the **Reopen closed tabs** link and selecting the tab, or tabs, that you want to reopen

To open a web page link in a new tab, press **Ctrl** as you click or right-click the link (or press and hold on the link) and select the **Open in new tab** option.

Right-click on a tab at the top of the browser window for a menu of options relating to the tab, even if it is not currently active.

To save the group of tabs for reuse at any time, click or tap on **Add to favorites** (see page 182) and select Add current tabs to favorites.

186

Zoom

Internet Explorer Zoom allows you to enlarge or reduce your view of a web page; it enlarges everything on the web page (image and text).

1 Select **View > Zoom** from the Menu bar to select options for viewing a web page

2 Select to zoom in or out or select an option for one of the predefined zoom levels (for example, 400%)

Reduce (zoom out) to get an overall view of a large web page. Enlarge (zoom in) to see the fine detail for one section of the page.

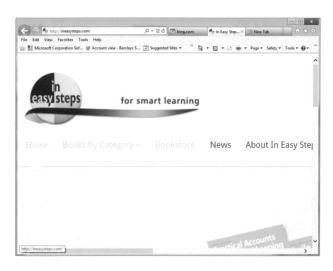

Select Custom to specify a magnification factor from 10% to 1000%.

Wheel Mouse Zoom

1 If you have a wheel mouse, hold down **Ctrl** and scroll the wheel to zoom in or out

Keyboard Zoom

1 Press **Ctrl −** to reduce, or **Ctrl +** to enlarge, in 25% increments. Press **Ctrl + *** to return to 100%

Print

In IE 11 on the Desktop, it is possible to print directly from the Command bar. To do this:

1 Select the **Print** button on the Command bar, and Internet Explorer automatically prints the current tab

Use Print Preview to see how the printed web page will appear.

1 With the required web page open, click the arrow next to the print button and select **Print Preview**

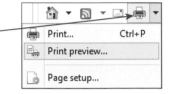

2 Note that the Shrink to Fit option is preselected in the Change Print Size box

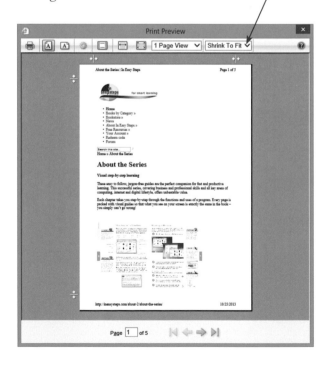

3 To illustrate the benefit of this, click the **down arrow** and select 100% and see how the print width changes

Don't forget

The print is automatically scaled to fit the paper size so that you will not find the right-hand edge chopped off.

Hot tip

Select the **Portrait** or **Landscape** buttons to quickly reorientate the print image.

Don't forget

You can select a print zoom factor from 30% to 200%, or enter a custom value. Full page view also offers easy-to-adjust margin handles.

10 Keeping in Touch

There are several
Windows 8.1 apps for
keeping in touch with people.
This chapter details how to
use the Mail, People, Skype
and Calendar apps.

Setting Up Mail

Email has become an essential part of everyday life, both socially and in the business world. Windows 8.1 accommodates this with the Mail app. This can be used to link to online services such as GMail and Outlook (the renamed version of Hotmail) and also other email accounts. To set up an email account with Mail:

Don't forget

You will also be prompted to add an account when you first access **Mail**, if you do not already have an account set up.

1 Click or tap on the **Mail** tile on the Start screen

2 Access the **Settings Charm**

3 Click or tap on the **Accounts** link

Settings

Mail
By Microsoft Corporation

Accounts

Help

About

Hot tip

The Other Account option in Step 5 can be used to add a non-web-mail account. This is usually a POP3 account and you will need your email address, username, password, and usually the incoming and outgoing email servers. If you do not know these they should be supplied by your email provider. They should also be available in the Accounts settings of the email app you want to add to the Mail app.

4 Click or tap on the **Add an account** button

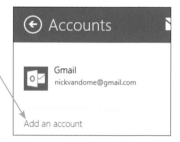

⬅ Accounts

Gmail
nickvandome@gmail.com

Add an account

5 Select the type of account to which you want to link to via the Mail app. This can be an online email account that you have already set up

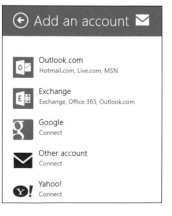

⬅ Add an account ✉

Outlook.com
Hotmail.com, Live.com, MSN

Exchange
Exchange, Office 365, Outlook.com

Google
Connect

Other account
Connect

Yahoo!
Connect

6 Enter your current login details for the selected email account and click or tap on the **Connect** button

You can add more than one account to the Mail app. If you do this you will be able to select the different accounts to view them within Mail.

7 Once it has been connected, the details of the account are shown under the Mail heading,

including the mailboxes within the account. Click or tap on the **Inbox** to view the emails within it

8 The list of emails appear in the left-hand pane Click or tap on a message to view it in the reading pane. Click or tap on this button to go back to the main window

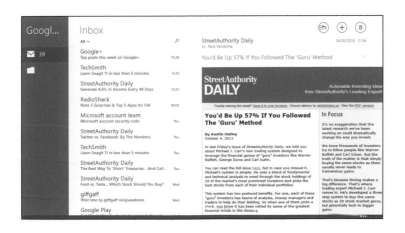

By default, the main window displays the item that was most recently selected in your Inbox.

Working with Mail

Once you have set up an account in the Mail app you can then start creating and managing your emails with it.

1 On the Inbox page, select an email and click or tap on this button to respond

| Reply |
| Reply all |
| Forward |

2 Select an email and click or tap on this button to delete it

Composing email

To compose and send an email message:

1 Click or tap on this button to create a new message

2 Click or tap in the **To** field and enter an email address

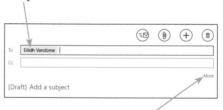

3 Click or tap on the **More** link to access options for blind copying and priority level

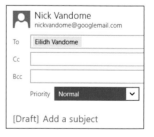

4 The email address can be in the format of myname@gmail.com or enter the name of one of your contacts in the People app and the email address will be entered automatically

Don't forget

Contacts that are added automatically as email recipients are taken from the People app, providing there is an email address connected to their entry.

5 Enter a subject heading and body text to the email

6 Click or tap on the **Attachments** button on the top toolbar in the new email window

7 Click or tap on a folder from which you want to attach the file

8 Select a file and click or tap on the **Attach** button

9 The file is shown in the body of the email

The bottom toolbar can also be accessed by pressing **WinKey** + **Z**.

10 Select an item of text or right-click or swipe up from the bottom of the screen to access the text formatting options

Emoticons (or smileys) can be accessed from the bottom toolbar, for insertion into emails.

11 Click or tap on this button to send the email

193

Sharing with Mail

It is great to share items via email, whether it is photos, music or video clips. There is no share function directly from Mail (although items can be added with the Attachments option) but items can be shared directly via email through their own apps and the Share Charm. To do this:

Beware

Items cannot be shared with the Share Charm from the Desktop.

Don't forget

When sharing photos via email, you have to select them first in the Mail app and then access the Share Charm.

1 Open an item you want to share, such as an image in the Photos app

2 Access the **Share Charm**

3 Select the **Mail** app as the method for sharing the item

4 The photo is attached to an email in the Mail app. Enter a recipient and subject and send as with a regular email

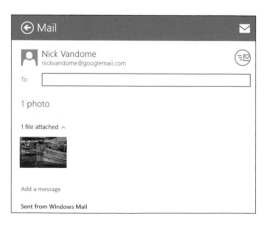

Searching within Mail

As you get more and more emails it may become difficult to find items within specific messages. To help find things, the Search Charm can be used, but it will search over a range of items, not just your email:

1 Open Mail and access the **Search Charm**

2 Enter a search word or phrase. Some of the results will include your emails (if they include the word or phrase) but other items will also be included

A more specific search option is to use the Search box within Mail itself:

1 Enter a word or phrase into the Search box at the top of the Inbox

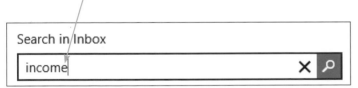

2 The results are displayed underneath the Inbox heading. Click or tap on an item to open the related email

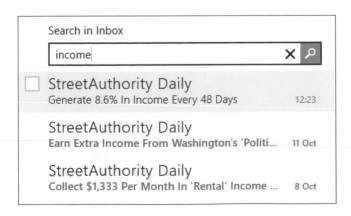

Hot tip

You can move an email to different mailboxes by selecting it and then accessing the bottom toolbar. Click or tap on the **Move** button and navigate to the mailbox that you want to use.

Finding People

An electronic address book is always a good feature to have on a computer and with Windows 8.1 this function is provided by the People app. This not only allows you to add your own contacts manually, you can also link to any of your online services, such as Facebook, Twitter and LinkedIn, and import the contacts that you have there. To do this:

1. Click or tap on the **People** tile on the Start screen

2. Click on the **Settings Charm** and click or tap on the **Accounts** link

3. The current accounts linked to the People app are listed. Click or tap on the **Add an account** button

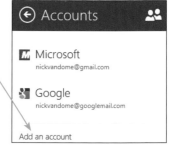

4. Select the account or service from which you would like to import your contacts

Hot tip

You can also select accounts to add to the People app from the Homepage when you first open it.

Don't forget

If your contacts are using Windows 8.1 you will be able to notify them of any updates through Facebook, Twitter or LinkedIn as long as they have these services added in their People app, and you are one of their contacts.

...cont'd

5 When you connect to the selected service you will be asked to grant Microsoft access to this account. Enter your details (for the account you are linking to) and click or tap on the **Ok, I'll Allow It** button

6 Complete any further registration windows for the service. In the final window click or tap on the **Done** button

7 The contacts are added under the **All contacts** section

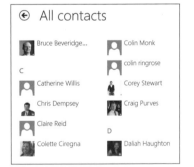

8 Click or tap on a contact to view their details

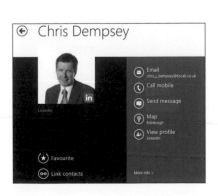

The icon on the contact's thumbnail indicates which service the contacts have been imported from, e.g. Facebook or LinkedIn.

Use the Search Charm to quickly find your contacts, particularly if you have a lot of them.

See page 199 for details about editing an entry.

...cont'd

Adding contacts manually

As well as importing contacts, it is also possible to enter them manually into the People app:

1 Right-click in the People window, or swipe up from the bottom of the window and click or tap on the **New** button

2 Enter details for the new contact, including name, email address and phone number

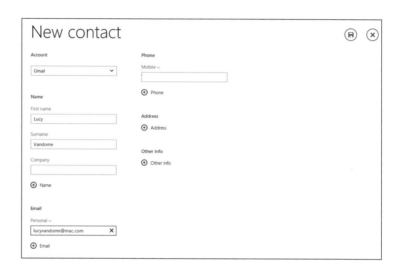

To delete a contact, click or tap on it to view the details. Then access the bottom toolbar and click or tap on the **Delete** button to remove it.

3 Click or tap on the plus sign next to a field to access additional options for that item

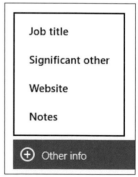

4 Click or tap on the **Save** button to create the new contact

5 Click or tap on a contact in the People window to view their details

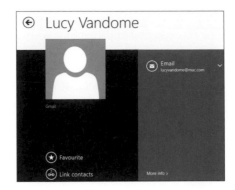

The photo for your own details within the People app is taken from the one provided for your Microsoft Account.

6 To edit a contact's details, right-click or swipe up from the bottom of the window and click or tap on the **Edit** button on the bottom toolbar. This brings up the same window in Step 2, on the previous page, where the details can be edited

7 Right-click or swipe up from the bottom of a contact's window and click or tap on the **What's new** button on the top toolbar to view any updates or notifications from your contacts. This could include Facebook, Twitter and LinkedIn updates

8 Click or tap on the **Me** button from the top toolbar to view your profile. If you have a Microsoft Account the details will come from this

If you select to edit your own details, you will be taken to your Microsoft Account profile on the Profile Live site.

9 Right-click or swipe up from the bottom of the window and click or tap on the **Edit** button on the bottom toolbar to edit your own profile

Chatting with Skype

Skype has become established as one of the premier services for free voice calls (to other Skype users) and instant messaging for text messages. It can now be incorporated into your Windows 8.1 experience and used to keep in touch with family, friends and work colleagues at home and around the world.

1 Skype can be downloaded, for free, from the Windows Store, if it is not already installed on your computer. Click or tap on the **Install** button

2 Click or tap on the Skype button on the Start screen or in the **All Apps** section

3 If you already have a Skype account, click or tap on the **I have a Skype account** button and enter your details. Otherwise, click or tap on the **I'm new to Skype** button and create an account

4 Once you have entered your Skype login details you will then be asked to merge your Skype account with your Microsoft one. Click or tap on the **Continue** button

Don't forget

Once you have merged your Microsoft and Skype accounts you will be able to sign in to your Skype account with your Microsoft account details.

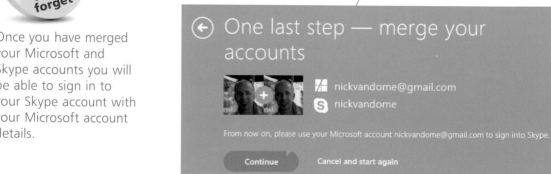

One last step — merge your accounts

nickvandome@gmail.com
nickvandome

From now on, please use your Microsoft account nickvandome@gmail.com to sign into Skype.

Continue   Cancel and start again

5 On the Skype Homepage recent calls and text message conversations are shown here

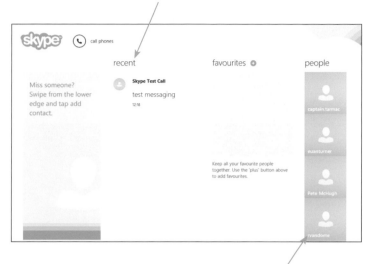

6 Skype contacts are shown here. Tap on one to start a voice call or text message

7 Click or tap on the green phone button to make a voice call

Don't forget

When you create a text conversation with one of your contacts in Skype, it will continue down the page as your respond to each other.

8 Click or tap here at bottom of the Skype window and enter a text message. Click or tap return to send the message

9 Right-click or swipe up from the bottom of the screen and tap on the **add contact** button to search for Skype contacts and add them under your People heading on the Homepage

Using the Calendar

The Calendar app can be used to include important events and reminders. To view the calendar:

1 Click or tap on the **Calendar** tile on the Start screen, or access it from All Apps

2 The calendar opens at the **What's next** view, which displays events that have been added to the calendar

3 Right-click or swipe up from the bottom of the screen to access the top Calendar toolbar. Click or tap on these buttons to view the calendar in different formats

4 Click, tap or swipe here to move backwards or forwards through the calendar

<October 2013 ˅>

5 Click or tap on the **What's next** button on the top toolbar to view the screen in Step 2

Don't forget

Accounts can be added to the Calendar app in the same way as for the Mail, Messaging and People apps.

Hot tip

To move between two months at a time, double-click or double-tap on the arrows in Step 3.

Adding events

Events can be added to the calendar and various settings can be applied to them such as recurrence and reminders.

1 Click or tap on a date or right-click or swipe up from the bottom of the screen and click or tap on the **New** button to create a new event

2 Enter details for the event including the location, the time and the duration. Enter a title for the event here and any message you want to add to it

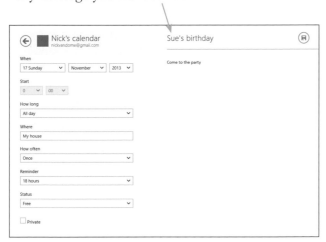

3 Click or tap on the **Start** field and enter a time for the event. Set its duration in the **How long** field

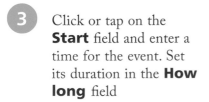

4 If **All day** is selected in the **How long** field the time in the **Start** field will be grayed-out

Reminders can be set for calendar events and these appear as pop-up boxes on the Start screen. They can also be set to appear on the Lock screen, in the **Notifications** section of the **PC settings**.

By default, there are preset calendars including birthdays and holidays. The colors of these can be changed from within the Calendar app by accessing the **Settings Charm** and selecting **Options**.

...cont'd

5 For a recurring event, click or tap in the **How often** box

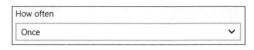

6 Select an option for the recurrence, such as **Every year** for a birthday

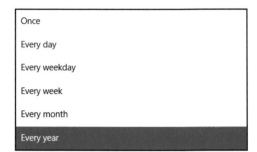

Hot tip

If you have connected the People app to your other accounts, such as Facebook or Twitter, the birthdays of your contacts from these sites will automatically be added to your calendar.

7 Click or tap on the **Save** button to save the event, or click or tap on the cross button to delete it

8 To delete an existing event, click or tap on it to open it

9 Right-click or swipe up from the bottom of the screen and click or tap on the **Delete** button

11 Networking

There is a built-in networking capability within Windows 8.1, allowing you to share a variety of items between two or more computers. This chapter shows how this can be done and how to set up the invaluable HomeGroup feature for file sharing.

The network adapter can be connected to the USB port, inserted in the PC Card slot or installed inside your computer.

Ethernet adapters connect to a network hub, switch or wired router. Wireless adapters connect through a wireless router or a combination of router/switch.

You may already have some of these elements in operation, if you have an existing network running a previous version of Windows.

Network Components

There are numerous possibilities for setting up a home network. To start with, there are two major network technologies:

- **Wired** – e.g. Ethernet, using twisted pair cables, to send data at rates of 10, 100 or 1000 Mbps (megabits per second)

- **Wireless** – using radio waves to send data at rates of 11 or 54 Mbps (or up to, in theory, 300 Mbps with the latest devices)

There is also a variety of hardware items needed:

- **Network adapter** – appropriate to the network type, with one for each computer in the network

- **Network controller** – one or more hub, switch or router, providing the actual connection to each network adapter

There is also the Internet connection (dial-up, DSL or cable) using:

- A modem connected to one of the computers

- A modem connected to the network

- Internet access incorporated into the router or switch

Set Up Your Network

The steps you will need, and the most appropriate sequence to follow, will depend on the specific options on your system. However, the main steps will include:

- Install network adapters in the computers, where necessary
- Set up or verify the Internet connection
- Configure the wireless router or access point
- Connect other computers and start up Windows on each PC

Install Hardware

If you need to install a wired or wireless network adapter, follow the instructions provided with the adapter. For example, to install the Linksys Wireless-N USB adapter:

1 Insert the CD provided and the setup program will start up automatically. Select the **Click Here to Start** button

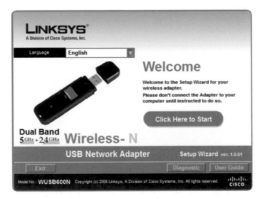

2 Follow the instructions (giving permission for access where requested) to complete the software installation

3 When prompted, attach the adapter to a USB port, via a cable if needed

4 When Windows has detected the wireless networks in your neighborhood, select your network and click or tap on the **Connect** button

With all the options and combinations that might be available, configuring the network could be complex. However, Windows 8.1 is designed to automate as much of the task as possible.

Depending on the AutoPlay settings, you may be prompted to run the installation option when you insert the CD.

Enter the security key for your wireless network when prompted.

Internet Connection

You do not actually require an Internet connection to set up a network, if all you want to do is share files and printers. However, in most cases the main purpose of the network is to share your connection to the Internet across several computers.

Verify your Connection

If you already have an Internet connection, open your web browser and go to a website that gets regularly updated (e.g. a news site). If the website opens with up-to-date entries and you don't get any error messages your connection is working.

Install Router

You can use a router with a DSL modem (an Internet gateway) to make an Internet connection available for sharing. This is usually set up on one computer, connected via an Ethernet cable or a USB cable. A configuration program may be provided on an installation CD or you can use your web browser.

If your router has been installed, Windows will automatically complete the connection to the Internet.

1 Open the browser and enter the IP address provided for the router, e.g. 192.168.1.254 or a similar local IP address

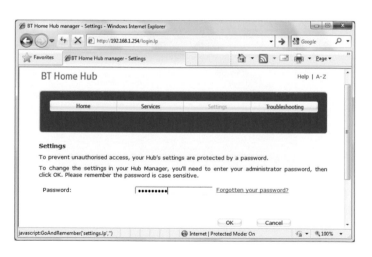

If you go to a website that stays relatively static, some of its web pages might be stored on your computer and will display correctly even if your connection is faulty.

2 Select Settings and enter the administrator user name (if required) and password, as provided by your ISP

You will be using the default ID and password for the particular equipment. While this can only be accessed from a direct local connection, you may feel more secure if you change the password.

3. Select **Admin Password**, then enter the old password and the new password and click to **Change password**

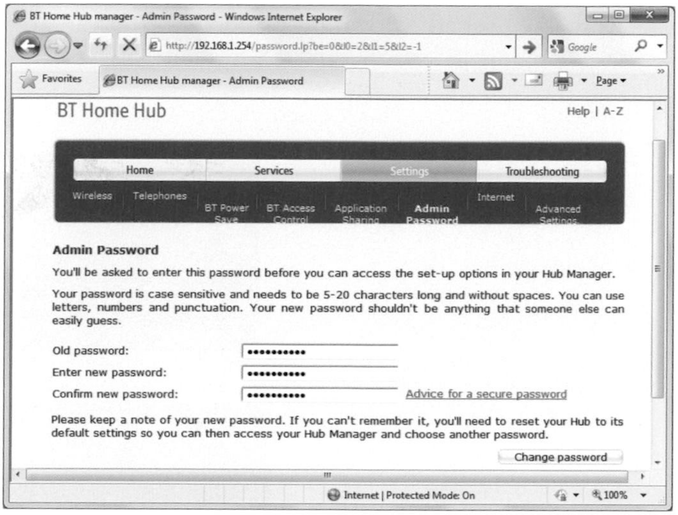
BT Home Hub manager - Admin Password - Windows Internet Explorer
http://192.168.1.254/password.lp?be=0&l0=2&l1=5&l2=-1
Favorites
BT Home Hub manager - Admin Password
BT Home Hub
Help | A-Z
Home
Services
Settings
Troubleshooting
Wireless
Telephones
BT Power Save
BT Access Control
Application Sharing
Admin Password
Internet
Advanced Settings
Admin Password
You'll be asked to enter this password before you can access the set-up options in your Hub Manager.
Your password is case sensitive and needs to be 5-20 characters long and without spaces. You can use letters, numbers and punctuation. Your new password shouldn't be anything that someone else can easily guess.
Old password:
Enter new password:
Confirm new password:
Advice for a secure password
Please keep a note of your new password. If you can't remember it, you'll need to reset your Hub to its default settings so you can then access your Hub Manager and choose another password.
Change password
Internet | Protected Mode: On
100%

Don't forget

The options offered will depend on the particular features of your router or gateway device, but they should, in principle, be similar.

4. Select **Wireless** to change the setup, for example by providing a new SSID (Service Set Identifier, the wireless network name) and choosing the encryption type and key

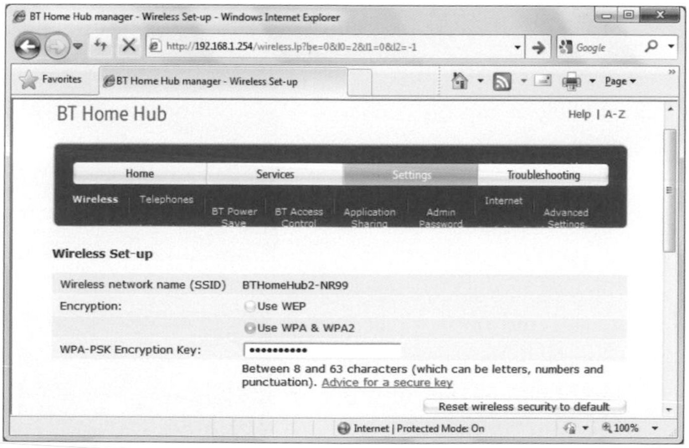
BT Home Hub manager - Wireless Set-up - Windows Internet Explorer
http://192.168.1.254/wireless.lp?be=0&l0=2&l1=0&l2=-1
Favorites
BT Home Hub manager - Wireless Set-up
BT Home Hub
Help | A-Z
Home
Services
Settings
Troubleshooting
Wireless
Telephones
BT Power Save
BT Access Control
Application Sharing
Admin Password
Internet
Advanced Settings
Wireless Set-up
Wireless network name (SSID)
BTHomeHub2-NR99
Encryption:
Use WEP
Use WPA & WPA2
WPA-PSK Encryption Key:
Between 8 and 63 characters (which can be letters, numbers and punctuation). Advice for a secure key
Reset wireless security to default
Internet | Protected Mode: On
100%

Beware

Do not use the default values for the parameters since these could be known to other people.

5. You can also change the channels used for the wireless communications, if you have problems with network range or speed, or interference from other devices

Discover Networks

Connect your computers to form your network, using Ethernet cables and adapters or by setting up your wireless adapters and routers. When you start up each computer, Windows 8.1 will examine the current configuration and discover any new networks that have been established since the last start up. You can check this, or connect manually to a network, from within the default settings from the Settings Charm. To do this:

1 Click or tap on the **Settings Charm** and click or tap on the **Network** button

2 Under the Wi-Fi heading, click or tap on one of the available networks

Beware

If your network is unavailable, for any reason, there will be a warning on the network button in Step 1.

3 Check on the **Connect automatically** box and click or tap on the **Connect** button to connect to the selected network

4 The selected network is shown as Connected. This is also shown on the Settings Charm in Step 1

Network and Sharing Center

The Network and Sharing Center within the Control Panel is where you can view settings for your network.

1 To open the Network and Sharing Center, access the Control Panel and click or tap on the **Network and Internet** link

2 Click or tap on the **Network and Sharing Center** link

3 Details of the current network are displayed in the Network and Sharing Center

4 Click or tap on the **Connections** link to see details of your Wi-Fi connection

5 The Wi-Fi information is displayed. Click or tap on the **Properties** button for more information

The Network and Sharing Center displays network settings and provides access to networking tasks for the computer.

In the Network and Sharing Center, click or tap on the **Set up a new connection or network** link to create a different network from the one currently in use.

Join the HomeGroup

A HomeGroup is a network function that enables a Windows 8.1 computer to connect to another Windows 8.1 machine (or Windows 7/8) and share content. There are different ways to join a HomeGroup, depending whether you connect from the Windows 8.1 interface, or through the Control Panel.

Connecting through the Windows 8.1 interface

To connect to a HomeGroup from the Windows 8.1 interface:

When you add a computer to your network, Windows 8.1 on that computer will detect that there is a HomeGroup already created.

1 Access the **Settings Charm** and click or tap on the **Change PC settings** button. Click or tap on the **HomeGroup** button under **Network**

2 Under the HomeGroup heading, click or tap on the **Create** button

3 Specify shared items. Drag the buttons to the right to enable items to be shared via the HomeGroup

Only computers on the same Home network and running the Windows 7 or 8 operating system (any edition) will be invited to join the HomeGroup.

4 Under the **Password** heading is a password.

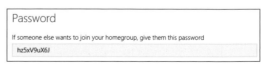

This has to be entered on any other computers that want to join the HomeGroup

...cont'd

Connecting through the Control Panel
To join a HomeGroup from the Control Panel:

1 Access **Network and Internet** in the Control Panel and click or tap on the **HomeGroup** link

2 Click or tap on the **Next** button to start setting up the HomeGroup

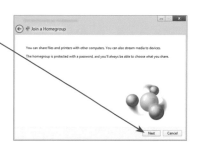

3 You can view details of the HomeGroup you want to join. Click or tap on the **Join now** button

4 Select the items that you want to share in the HomeGroup and click or tap on the **Next** button

5 Enter the password that has to be provided from the other computer

6 Once you have joined the HomeGroup you will be able to share your files on the other computer and vice versa

HomeGroup applies to any user with an account on the computer, so if a different user logs on, the associated files will also be accessible.

Windows generates the password when the HomeGroup is created (see previous page). If you forget the password, you can find it in the Control Panel on any computer already joined to the HomeGroup.

If there is a printer to be shared, Windows 8.1 will automatically take the action needed to make it available on the network.

213

Sharing Files and Folders

There are different ways in which you can share items once a HomeGroup has been set up:

1 Open the File Explorer and select the **HomeGroup** in the Library pane and click or tap on the **Share libraries** button in the Share section of the File Explorer

The Share section in File Explorer is accessed from the Scenic Ribbon.

2 Select the items that you want to share with the HomeGroup. This will be done automatically, i.e. if you share Pictures then all of the items in the Pictures library will be shared, as will new ones that are added

3 To share a specific item, select it in the File Explorer and click or tap on the **HomeGroup** button in the Share section

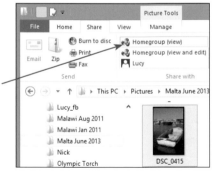

4 Select the HomeGroup in the Navigation pane of the File Explorer Library pane to view the shared item in Step 3

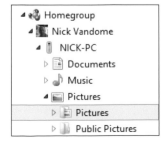

Sharing Settings

Within the Network and Sharing Center there are also options for specifying how items are shared over the network, not just in the HomeGroup. To select these:

1 Open the Network and Sharing Center and click or tap on the **Change advanced sharing settings** link

> Change advanced sharing settings

2 Select sharing options for different networks, including private, guest or public and all networks. Options can be selected for turning on network discovery so that your computer can see other computers on the network, and file and printer sharing

Don't forget

If you are sharing over a network you should be able to access the Public folder on another computer (providing that network discovery is turned on). If you are the administrator of the other computer you will also be able to access your own home folder, although you will need to enter the required password for this.

3 Click or tap on these buttons to view the options for each network category

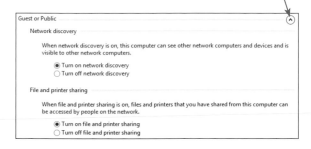

215

Sharing a Printer

When you join a HomeGroup, Windows may detect a shared printer. However, the software drivers required may not be installed on this machine. To make the printer available:

1 Click or tap on the **Install printer** button

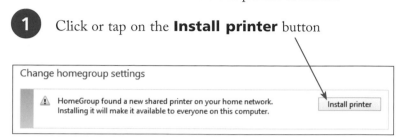

2 Click or tap on the **Install driver** button, to confirm you trust the computer and network sharing the printer

3 The driver files are copied to your computer

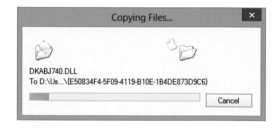

Beware

If you are using a shared printer, the computer from where you are sharing it has to be turned on in order for you to use the printer.

4 The shared printer is added to the Devices and Printers section in the Control Panel

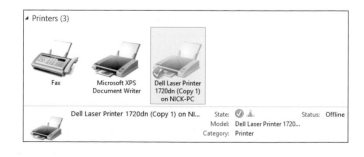

View Network Components

You can also view the network components in the network in File Explorer. To do this:

1 Open File Explorer and click or tap on the **Network** link

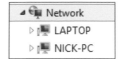

2 To view the shared items offered by a particular computer, for example the Nick-PC, double-click or tap on the associated icon

3 Double-click or tap to view the contents of networked folders

The Public folder on your own computer can be used to make items available to other users on the network.

Don't forget

Public files and folders plus those belonging to the currently-active user are available for access. Items can be copied here for sharing purposes.

Network Troubleshooting

1 Open the Network and Sharing Center and select **Troubleshoot problems**

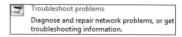

Troubleshoot problems
Diagnose and repair network problems, or get troubleshooting information.

2 Windows searches online for troubleshooting packs

Windows 8.1 provides several troubleshooters to resolve common problems with networks. They are downloaded, so you always get the most up-to-date help.

3 Select, for example, Shared Folders and follow the prompts to describe and hopefully resolve the problems

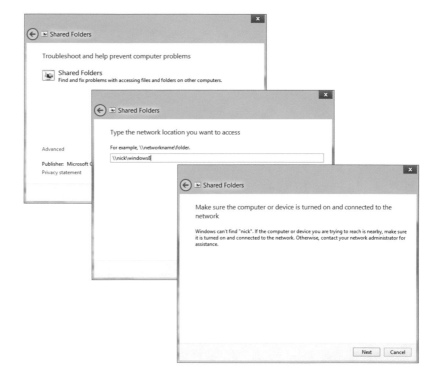

In this case, a problem accessing a folder on another computer is quickly resolved as a typing error, when Windows says it cannot find "windows8" but detects the similar folder name "Windows 8.1" (with a space before 8).

12 System and Security

Windows 8.1 includes tools to enhance the security and performance of your computer. It helps you to maintain your hard drive, protects your computer from malicious software and keeps your system up-to-date.

System Properties

There are several ways to open the System Properties, and view information about your computer:

1 Access the **Control Panel, System and Security** and then click or tap on the **System** category

2 Press the **WinKey** + the **Pause/Break** keys

3 Right-click **This PC** in the File Explorer and select **Properties** from the menu

4 Right-click in the bottom left-hand corner and select **System** from the contextual menu

The main panel provides the Windows 8.1 edition, processor details, memory size, computer and network names, and Windows 8.1 activation status. There are also links to the Device Manager and to more advanced settings.

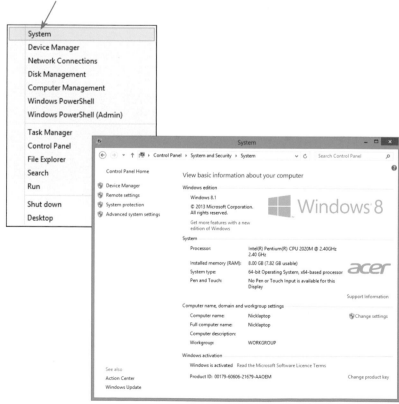

...cont'd

Device Manager

1 Select **Device Manager**, to list all of the hardware components that are installed on your computer

2 Select the ▷ symbol to expand that entry to show details

3 Select the ◢ symbol to collapse the expanded entry

4 Double-click or tap any device to open its properties

You may be prompted for an administrator password or asked for permission to continue, when you select some Device Manager entries.

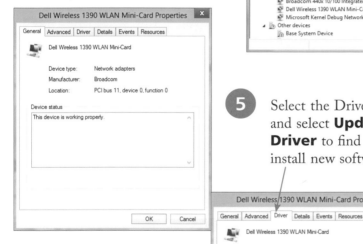

5 Select the Driver tab and select **Update Driver** to find and install new software

6 Select **Disable** to put the particular device offline. The button changes to Enable, to reverse the action

Click the **Roll Back Driver** button to switch back to the previously-installed driver for that device, if the new one fails.

Clean Up Your Disk

1 In the File Explorer, right-click on **OS (C:)** and click or tap on the **Properties** link

2 Click or tap on the **Disk Clean-up** button

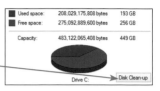

3 Disk Clean-up scans the drive to identify files that can be safely removed

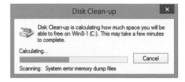

4 All of the possible files are listed by category, and the sets of files recommended to be deleted are marked with a tick symbol

5 Make changes to the selections, clicking **View Files** if necessary to help you choose

6 Select the button **Clean up system files**, to include these also, then select **OK**

7 Deleted files will not be transferred to the Recycle Bin, so confirm that you do want to permanently delete all of these files. The files will be removed and the disk space will become available

Don't forget

You can have more than one hard disk on your computer, or you can divide one hard disk into several partitions, with separate drive letters.

222

...cont'd

When a file is written to the hard disk, it may be stored in several pieces in different places. This fragmentation of disk space can slow down your computer. Disk Defragmenter rearranges the data so the disk will work more efficiently.

1 In the File Explorer, right-click on **OS (C:)** and click or tap on the **Properties** link

2 Select the **Tools** tab and click or tap on the **Optimize** button

3 The process runs as a scheduled task, but you can select a drive and select **Analyze** to check out a new drive

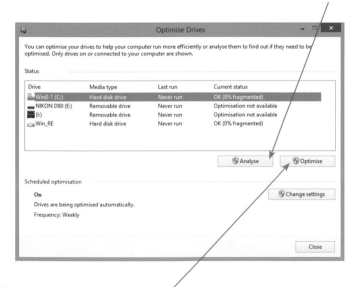

4 Click or tap the **Optimize** button to process the selected disk. This may take from several minutes to several hours to complete, depending on the size and state of the disk, but you can still use your computer while the task is running

Don't forget

The spellings are localized.

Hot tip

Only disks that can be fragmented are shown. These can include USB drives that you add to your system.

Windows Update

Windows Update manages updates to Windows 8.1 and other Microsoft products. Applying updates can prevent or fix problems, improve the security or enhance performance, so Windows Update can be set up to install important updates automatically. To review your settings for Windows Update:

1 Select **Control Panel**, **System and Security** and select **Windows Update**

Alternatively, you can click **Windows Update** from Action Center.

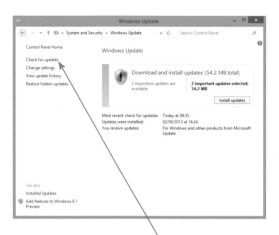

Click or tap on **View update history** to see the changes that have previously been applied to your system.

2 To see if there are any updates that are waiting to be downloaded and applied, select **Check for updates**

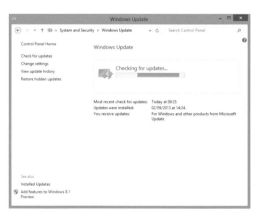

See page 226 for details about changing the settings for how Windows Update functions.

3 If there are updates, click or tap on **Install updates** to download and apply them immediately, or wait for Windows Update to install them at the scheduled time

...cont'd

Updating with the Metro interface

In Windows 8.1 updates can also be installed from the PC settings in the Metro interface. To do this:

1 Access the **Settings Charm** and click or tap on the **Change PC settings** button

2 Click or tap on the **Update and recovery** button and select the **Windows Update** option

3 Click or tap on the **View details** button to see details of any updates that are waiting to be installed

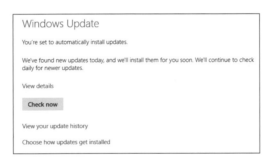

4 Click or tap on the **Install** button to install the selected updates. Click or tap on the **Check now** button in Step 3 to see if there are any more available updates

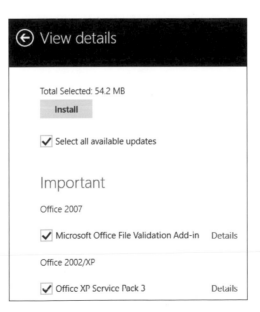

The **Recovery** option under the **Update and recovery** heading can be used to refresh your computer without affecting your files and also removing everything and reinstalling Windows.

225

Change Settings

From the Metro interface the settings can be changed by clicking or tapping on the **Choose how updates get installed** button from Step 3 on the previous page and make the required selections.

1 Open Windows Update and select **Change settings**

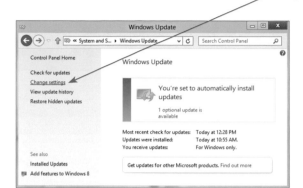

2 The recommended option is to install updates automatically. This assumes a broadband link

Beware

You may need to turn off Windows Update completely, by choosing **Never check for updates**, when you are traveling where the Internet connections available are unsuitable for downloading.

3 You can specify to download updates in the background, but pick your own time to install them

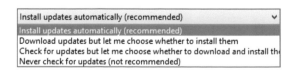

4 Alternatively, you can have Windows Update check for updates and alert you when they are available, but choose for yourself when to both download and install them

Back Up and Recover Data

1 Open **Control Panel** and select **Save backup copies of your files with File History**, in the **System and Security** category

2 The first time you do this, you can select a drive such as an external hard drive or a network drive. Click or tap on the **Turn on** button to back up copies of your files

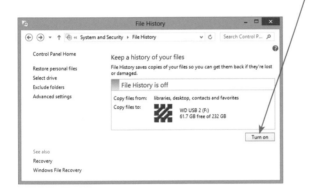

To make sure you do not lose the files stored on your computer, you should back them up regularly. Windows will help you set up automatic backups.

3 Details of the backup are displayed here

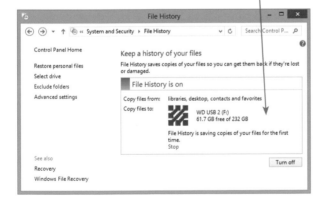

You can create a system image and also back up data files in the libraries and other folders on your system.

4 Click or tap on the **Run now** link to perform another backup

System Restore

Windows 8.1 takes snapshots of the system files before any software updates are applied, or in any event once every seven days. You can also create a snapshot manually. The snapshots are known as Restore Points and are managed by System Restore.

1 Open **System** under **System and Security** and select **System protection**

2 Select the **Create** button, to create a restore point manually

3 Provide a title for the restore point and click **Create**

4 The required data is written to disk and the manual restore point is set up

228

Using Restore Points

The installation of a new app or driver software may make Windows 8.1 behave unpredictably or have other unexpected results. Usually, uninstalling the app or rolling back the driver will correct the situation. If this does not fix the problem, use an automatic or manual restore point to reset your system to an earlier date when everything worked correctly.

...cont'd

1 Select **System Protection** and click the **System Restore** button

System Restore...

2 By default this will offer to undo the most recent change. This may fix the problem

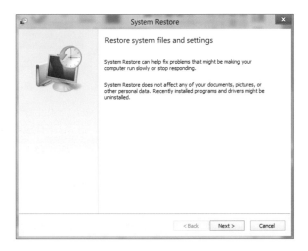

You can also run System Restore from Safe Mode, the troubleshooting option. Start up the computer and press **F8** repeatedly as your computer reboots, to display the boot menu, then select **Safe Mode**.

3 Otherwise, click **Choose a different restore point**, and pick a suitable time

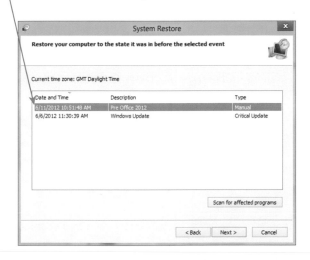

If the selected restore point does not resolve the problem, you can try again, selecting another restore point.

4 Follow the prompts to restart the system using system files from the selected date and time

Action Center

The Action Center monitors security and system maintenance issues and delivers alerts for features such as Windows Backup.

1 Move the mouse over the Action Center icon on the Notifications section of the Taskbar to see the status. If a problem is detected, the icon is marked with a white cross in a red circle

2 Click or tap on the icon for more details, then select **Open Action Center**

230

In the Action Center you can also change User Account Control settings and Windows Updates.

3 You can solve the problems from the Action Center, or click or tap **Change Action Center settings** to adjust the alerts

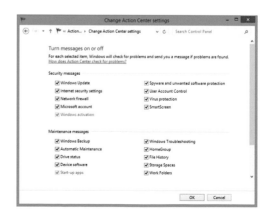

Windows Firewall

1 Open Control Panel, select the System and Security category and select **Windows Firewall**

2 Select **Turn Windows Firewall on or off** to customize settings for private (home and work) and public networks

3 Select **Allow an app or feature through Windows Firewall**, to view the allowed apps

Allow an app or feature through Windows Firewall

4 Select **Allow another app**, if you need to Add an app

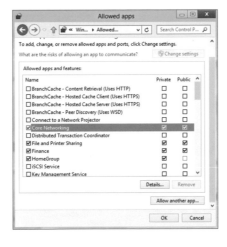

The Windows Firewall can be used to provide a level of protection against malicious software and viruses.

Firewall is on by default in Windows 8.1, but you can turn it off if you have another Firewall installed and active. Note that if you have a router with a built-in firewall, you still need the Windows 8.1 Firewall (or other firewall) on your computer.

Only add apps to the allowed list if you are advised to do so by a trusted advisor.

Malware Protection

1 Open Control Panel, type *Defender* in the Search box and select **Windows Defender**

2 Click or tap on the **Settings** tab and adjust settings such as real-time protection, exclusions and advanced settings

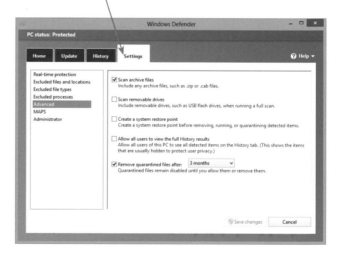

3 For an immediate check, select the **Home** tab and click or tap on the **Scan now** button

Scan now

Index

235

O

P

R

U

V

W

Z